How to Release the Burdens You Were Never Meant to Carry

SOUL CRUSHERS

HOW TO RELEASE THE BURDENS YOU WERE NEVER MEANT TO CARRY

JESSE BARNETT

Soulcrushers: How to Release the Burdens You Were Never Meant to Carry

Published by Flightwords Press

Cover design and interior typography by Laura Schaeffer

ISBN: 978-1-7364796-0-5. First edition.

I DEDICATE THIS BOOK
TO THOSE WHOSE BACKS ARE BENT,
WHOSE COUNTENANCE IS WEARY,
AND WHOSE HOPE IS FRAGILE.
MAY YOU SOON FIND A LIGHT AT THE END
OF THE TUNNEL AND THE ROAD
AHEAD TO BE EASY.

CONTENTS

FOREWORD

2020. What a year.

I've got to be honest. I thought it would go a little differently. I used to joke that all the best stuff in my life happened in the even years. I graduated college (twice!) in even years; I got married in an even year; my kids were born in even years. In general, even years just seem to work out better for me.

And then 2020 hit.

I would imagine you can relate. Nothing went according to plan. Thanks to the global pandemic of COVID19, we became used to shortages of toilet paper and antibacterial everything, wearing masks in public, social distancing, lack of travel, remote working, kids doing school online, and a general unease about everything.

It felt like everything was out of control, and yet when January 2021 came into sight, we felt like we were about to turn a corner.

A new year was on the way, and with it, a chance to become better.

We can't control what's going on in the world, but that's not really what this book's about.

The message of this book is that there are certain things that shape you that take place on the inside.

They don't care where you live, if you are cooped up inside your home, if you wear a mask or not. These *Soulcrushers* are with you every single day, and only you can determine whether or not you want to pick them up and bear their weight.

Today, I want to challenge you to take a look at what you're carrying into your future. Most of us need to lighten our load a bit or we're not going to make it. Or we'll make it but we won't make it as far as we should.

Although this book deals with some deep issues, I've tried to keep the tone encouraging and light. I don't take myself too seriously, but I am serious about becoming a better version of myself—the version that God designed me to be.

This means I must continually work on my soul and remove the things that weigh it down, replacing them with something better. It's work, but it's good work, and the benefits far outweigh the costs.

I hope you'll join me on this journey and it makes this year the best year of your life.

Even if it's not an even one.

Thanks for joining me on the journey.

Jesse

SHAKEDOWN

I know we just met, but I want you to humor me for a moment.

If you are in a chair I want you to lean back against the backrest. If you are in a bed or on a couch I want you to let your head sink into the pillows or cushion. Now close your eyes and take a deep breath—a good old "in through the nose, out through the mouth" type of a deep breath.

Now do it again.

I want you to pay close attention to the muscles around your eyes and forehead and your shoulders and neck. How are they feeling? Unless you are reading this on a warm, sunny beach somewhere, there's probably a little bit of tension there.

Try tensing those muscles for a moment like you are trying to squint your eyes or shrug your shoulders. Then let out that tension. Did your muscles relax, or are they still tight?

If you are like most people, you carry that tightness and anxiety with you all the time.

It's a constant reminder that you have a hundred things on your mind all at once and you have no idea how to handle them. What's worse, they never seem to go away and new problems get added every day.

Sound familiar? You're not alone.

Add in a global pandemic that doesn't seem to want to go away and it's no wonder we're tense.

This book isn't going to cure all your worries and fears and doubts and anxieties. No book can. We live in a world that is a tough place. For each innovation that makes our life easier, there are ten more things that make it more difficult.

So don't expect me to be able to solve all your problems. I can't. What I can do is help you think about them in a different way and hopefully give you the means to work through some common burdens that most of us carry.

The Myth of the Overpacker

I live outside of Atlanta, Georgia. It's about an hour and a half drive away from the start of the Appalachian Trail. The AT, as it's often referred to by hikers, is a trail 2,200 miles long that starts in Springer Mountain, GA and terminates at Mount Katahdin, ME. For many people, trekking the AT is a lifetime pursuit. While some diehards will trek the entire trail at one time, most people do sections at a time, a process called "section-hiking."

At the start of the Appalachian Trail hikers start out full of energy and brimming with confidence in their fortitude and abilities. They spend months researching the supplies they'll need and collecting their boots, clothes, food, and packs. Like any traveler, a hiker on the AT has to know what is vital and what is unnecessary.

In Neels Gap, Georgia there's a little store called Mountain Crossings. It's the only place on the over 2,100 miles of the Appalachian Trail where the trail passes through a building. This store is 30.7 miles north of where the trail starts. This stacked stone building was built by the Civilian Conservation Corps in the 1930s, nearly torn down in the 1970s, and reimagined as a store in 1983.

Now it has become a rite of passage for hikers of the AT where the Mountain Crossings staff is famous for one thing: the Shakedown. Most new hikers make the same mistake—they buy a big backpack and stuff it to the gills with everything they think they'll need for the journey. Then they include a few extras that they don't really need but would love to have to make their hike more enjoyable. This includes things like favorite ceramic coffee mugs, hardback books for reading, and extra footwear.

As you can imagine, after thirty miles of hiking over hilly terrain the extra weight adds up. You feel it in your legs, shoulders, back, and those little muscles you didn't even realize you had when you started. Even the most comfortable pack can become a burden when it's overloaded and shouldered for eight to twelve hours a day. By the time these overly optimistic hikers get to Mountain Crossings, they are starting to doubt their stamina.

This is when the friendly staff jumps in and performs a Shakedown.

This process takes anywhere from one to four hours (depending on the overall ambitiousness of the hiker). As they rest their weary feet, the Shakedown begins with a purge of all non-essential items. These items can either be shipped home or left at the store.

After their load is lightened to just what they need for the trek, they can continue up the trail and onto their adventure. Without a good Shakedown, many of these hikers will give up and quit, never reaching their goal and forever wondering what might have been.

Soulcrushers

In the journey of life, you could probably use a good Shakedown from time to time.

Doing life is a lot like taking a hike on a mountain trail. We pack everything we think we need at the start of our journey. This includes things like our vision for the world we want to create, our educational goals, our perfect spouse, our ideal job, our dream house, our maxed out 401k, and our lofty dreams of retirement.

We then add things like a spouse, who like us is imperfect. And kids who bring us equal parts of joy, stress, and worry about their future. We build on that with a house payment that stretches our finances and additional education to help us get ahead with our more challenging, but higher paying job, and all the stress that comes along with it.

Then we have a bad habit of picking up some heavy burdens that *really* weigh us down. These are things like fear, doubt, anger, bitterness, worry, unforgiveness, jealousy, selfishness, pride, disappointment, and hopelessness.

You probably don't want to hear it, but I'm sure you struggle with more than one of these. You may even have something in your pack that isn't on my list. These burdens affect us all and are a byproduct of living in a fallen and broken world.

These burdens are what I call *Soulcrushers.*

Here's the ironic part. The worst thing about Soulcrushers is they are burdens you were *never meant to carry*, yet every day you pick up your pack, shoulder the load, and struggle through life—many times not even knowing what is weighing you down.

It's Time for a Shakedown

My goal for this book is simple—I want to help you by giving you a shakedown. I want to give you the tools you need to be good at life, and part of that process is getting rid of the burdens that weigh you down.

Here are the most common and the ones we'll deal with in this book:

- **FEAR** — robs you of your confidence and causes you to live life timidly.
- **DOUBT** — takes away your courage and assurances you know to be true.
- **ANGER** — festers until it consumes you and cripples you for life.
- **BITTERNESS** — becomes a byproduct of anger that captures your joy.
- **WORRY** — takes away your focus on today and turns it into anxiety over tomorrow.
- **UNFORGIVENESS** — makes you hang on to past wounds and relive them over and over.
- **JEALOUSY** — becomes a constant comparison where you can't be happy for others.
- **SELFISHNESS** — causes you to overlook others and only focus on yourself.
- **PRIDE** — convinces you that you are better than others and deserve more.
- **DISAPPOINTMENT** — causes you to look at the world in a negative light.
- **HOPELESSNESS** — causes you to want to give up.

It's important to remember that shakedowns hurt at first. I'm sure those hikers don't want to give up their "World's Best Dad" coffee mug or their "Guide to

Plants and Bugs that Will Kill You on the Appalachian Trail" reference guide.

Even looking at this list you may feel daunted and discouraged. Please don't. Push through that feeling and have confidence you can come through better on the other side. One of my gifts is the ability to tackle tough subjects like this with heart, humor, and hope. That's what we'll do together.

If you want to become the best version of yourself, to live with a soul that is light, airy, and hopeful then you have to make a choice. You can continue to pick up your overloaded backpack, drag all these things that you think you need and can't live without, or lighten your load and finish the journey.

You've likely carried some of your burdens for *years*. Maybe it's something a friend said in anger that you can't forget. You pull those words out of your pack and replay them over and over in your mind. Perhaps it's a familiar worry over making ends meet that keeps you from falling asleep at night as you review your finances and think about the bills. Maybe it's a root of bitterness because of a person who didn't live up to your expectations (expectations, by the way, that they probably didn't know existed) that poisons your outlook on relationships. It could be a lingering doubt that robs you of your ability to trust others and live a full life.

Whatever Soulcrushers are weighing you down, now is the time to unstrap your pack and let your burden crash to the ground. At first, you may miss it, but once you learn to live without it, you'll never look back.

So, are you ready to lighten that load, and live the good life you've been missing out on?

I hope so. Let's get started now.

1

HERE IS THE WORLD.
BEAUTIFUL AND TERRIBLE
THINGS WILL HAPPEN.
DON'T BE AFRAID.

Frederick Buechner

Think about the kind of person you are right now in this moment of your life.

I'm not talking about the you you show the world when you are in public. Chances are *that* you isn't the real you anyway. Like an airbrushed picture fails to capture the essence of the subject, *that* you probably does not show its insecurities and doubts, anxieties and burdens, and worries and fears. *That* you has it all together—not a hair out of place, gut sucked in, ready smile, and a ready answer for any question.

But if you are being honest, that you is probably a little bit phony.

The real you is probably self-conscious, timid, unpolished, filled with doubt, wanting to be accepted and loved, and scared of what people really think about you. This is the you that stays hidden most of the time.

Now think about the person you *want* to be. The real you. The authentic you. The *you* God made you to be. The *you* you'd show the world if you weren't afraid. What is this you like?

More importantly, what are the differences between those two yous?

Far too many people let the fear of what others think stop them from being authentic and true to themselves. As author John Eldredge puts it, they create a "fig leaf" just like Adam and Eve did to hide themselves away and cover up their rough edges.

Unfortunately, you can't hide from who you are.

And life is a burden as long as you keep who you are hidden.

Go Along to Get Along?

I recently saw a guy wearing a T-shirt that said, *"Sorry I'm late. I don't really want to be here."* It's funny, but it's also refreshingly honest. How many times do you do something you have no desire to do simply because it's the right thing to do? Someone expects it of you, so you go along, too afraid to do or say what you really want because it might put you in an uncomfortable position.

In the same way, we have an idea of what the world expects us to be. You know what you are supposed to say (or not). You know how you are supposed to behave (or not). You know these things because they are drilled into you from an early age. In fact, fear as a motivator is often used in education, manners, and work.

Don't do this, or bad things will happen.

It's effective, but that fear of not performing or living up to the expectations of others gets ingrained in your subconscious and becomes a sort of self-imposed prison. You cease to be real, because being real is wrong. It might offend. It might upset. It might make you different. So you color inside the lines; you work nine to five at a job that is unfulfilling, and you don't live the life you want to live—the life you *were created* to live—because you are afraid.

This is so far from the life God wants for you that it breaks my heart.

The One and Only You

There is only one you. Let that sink in for a minute.

What makes the Mona Lisa, the Statue of Liberty, the Sistine Chapel, the Grand Canyon, the North Star, Beethoven's Fifth Symphony, and that freckle on your left arm unique?

Give up?

The answer is there's only one of them in all the world.

Are there other paintings besides the Mona Lisa? Of course, but there's only one with that mischievous smile that art critics and amateurs alike have spent centuries trying to understand. There are also replicas of the Statue of Liberty, but there is only one that welcomed weary immigrants to the Land of Opportunity after leaving the only home they'd ever known and sailing across an uncertain sea in a crowded ship to a future that wasn't mapped out.

Likewise the Grand Canyon, the North Star, Beethoven's Fifth. Each one is unique. Similar to its contemporaries to be sure, but unique nonetheless.

So it is with you. The one and only you. You may have a doppelgänger somewhere, but there's only one you with all your hopes and dreams and quirks and eccentricities. You are uniquely wired, handmade, knit together by the inspiration and the imagination of God himself.

Wow. Let that sink in.

The God that *made* you to *be* you expects you to do just that: Be You.

He doesn't want you to be anyone else, so why are you living in fear?

THE DOWNSIDE OF FEAR

Fear is a thief and a liar. It steals your joy and robs you of your dreams. It's also a bully. Like the big kid in your high school that terrorized the nerds, fear waits in the corner until it sees something it can't have and then pounces.

But what you need to know is that fear can also be a tool. It can drive you to do heroic things. It can push you to the crucible moment you need that heats you to a boiling point and pushes you to say, "Enough!" and make a move that changes your life.

But before you can defeat your enemy, you must *understand* your enemy. Rosa Parks said, "I have learned over the years that when one's mind is made up, this diminishes fear; knowing what must be done does away with fear." When you understand your fears, they are diminished, and this gives you the courage to overcome them and remove them from your life forever.

Here are some truths about fear that you need to understand:

Fear is a Lack of Faith

Where do you place your faith? Is it in your strengths, talents, and abilities? Is it in your family, your work, or your hobbies? Is it in God and his purpose and plan for you?

Fear forms when you shift your faith from God and put it in something you are afraid of. In essence, you are saying that what you fear is bigger than God and stronger than you are. It may be stronger than you, but it can never be bigger than God.

The first thing to understand about fear is that it stems from your faith. You have faith in something or someone. Everyone does. Where you put that faith will determine your ability to overcome and defeat your fear. If you have faith that your fear is bigger than you, it will run wild and control your life. If you have faith that God is bigger than your fear, you can begin to work through it and let go of this burden you are carrying.

Fear Focuses on a Future that Rarely Happens

Have you ever noticed how in the movies when something scary is about to happen the music changes and becomes more intense? You watch the character on the screen, and you're screaming, "Don't go through that door! That's where the bad guy is!"

Wouldn't it be nice if life had a warning soundtrack too?

One of the tricks that fear plays on you is that it convinces you that the worst is yet to come. It plays with your mind and manipulates you into constantly waiting for the other shoe to drop. So you live with one eye always on an uncertain future, and that type of living takes your eyes off of your present.

The lie is that what you most fear rarely happens. It's not that it couldn't happen; it's just that fear magnifies the little things into big things and stops you from embracing life.

Fear Focuses Your Attention on Factors Outside of Your Control

A quick Google search will reveal a lot of crazy ways that people have died: falling out of an "unbreakable" skyscraper window, getting attacked by monkeys, or driving your Segway scooter off a cliff.

I'm fairly certain that you didn't wake up worrying about any of these things happening to you today. Could they happen? Of course. Are they likely? Not very. Especially now that I've warned you that they could.

But fear has an uncanny knack for shifting your attention to circumstances far beyond your control. It somehow causes all the truth and logic to fly out the window and replaces it with what-ifs, maybes, and worse case scenarios.

But when you learn to recognize that thinking for what it is, you can halt your fears and put a stop to it. My friend Chet is a counselor, and he says that your thoughts are like a spiral. If you aren't careful those thoughts can spiral down, like water swirling around a drain. When you see your thoughts spiraling down you have to make a choice to halt that kind of thinking and focus on what you can control.

You can't control everything. No one can. But when you focus on the things you can control and do your best at those things, you limit the effect of fear and rob it of its power over you.

Fear Divides and Conquers

If I asked you to list your greatest strengths and assets right now, what would you say?

Even if you have self-esteem that is tattered and shredded, if you are honest, you'll be able to point to some of your strengths. You may be kind, joyful, forthright, a champion for the underdog, loyal, optimistic, an encourager, a hard worker. The list goes on and on, but fear tries to convince you otherwise. It gives too much credit to itself and discounts all of your strengths that make you you.

My wife loves Winnie the Pooh, and one of her favorite quotes from author A.A. Milne's book is, *"You are braver than you believe, stronger than you seem, smarter than you think, and loved more than you know."*

So it is with you—but fear doesn't want you to think about that. It convinces you that you are a coward, that you are weak, that you are dumb, and that you are unlovable. Don't listen to the lies! Don't let fear divide you from what you know to be true: God made the one and only you, and he doesn't make mistakes.

CRUSHING FEAR

Fear isn't all bad. Fear keeps you from doing stupid things that are detrimental to your life and health. Used properly, fear can become a tool that doesn't weigh you down, but actually makes you better at life.

Fear Can Be an Incredible Motivator

I want to be a great husband, a great father, a talented and thriving writer, a loyal friend, a good son and brother, an honorable man, and a faithful follower of Christ.

But I know the selfishness and sin that is in my own heart, and frankly, it scares me.

What if I fail as a husband, dad, writer, friend, son, brother, man, and Christian? What will the world say? What will those who love me say? What will I say?

That fear of not measuring up is a powerful motivator to do the right things. It makes me want to fight and work on my marriage. It makes me strive to do everything possible to be the dad my kids love and respect. It drives me to keep writing words that inspire and encourage. It reminds me to pursue uplifting friendships and check in on my brother and sister and mom. It pushes me to consider my legacy, and, most importantly, it makes me constantly evaluate my walk with Jesus and my lifelong journey of growing more like him every day.

Your fear can be an incredible motivator. Think about the life you want to live and the legacy you want to leave. Then use your fears to push you to make better decisions and choices that drive you towards that outcome.

Fear Can Push You to Do More Than You Thought Possible

I read somewhere that you should do something that scares you every day. It's an interesting thought. How many times do you take the safe road that's unchallenging?

If you are a guy and you grew up when I did, you remember the terror of calling a girl's house to talk to her or ask her on a date. Back in the olden days, when phones were something you hung on a wall or sat on the kitchen counter, you never knew who would pick it up when you called.

Murphy's Law says that it would be the girl's dad, and that was a terrifying prospect. My dad would answer the phone with a gruff, "Barnett." That's it. No "hello", no "This is Mr. Barnett speaking." Just one-word that said, "You're calling me at my house; what do you want?" I can only imagine the terror my sister's boyfriends must have felt.

But that rite of passage of calling a girl, surviving her father, and getting the date made us realize that we were stronger and braver than we thought.

Overcoming fear is like that. It's like getting on a roller coaster for the first time and being terrified of the click-click-click of the cars on the track during the initial climb. It's powerful at first, but once you finish the ride you feel stronger, better, and tougher than you did before.

Fear Can Be the Crucible that Drives you to Greatness

At the end of your life, what do you want to be said of you?

Perhaps even more important, what do you want to be *thought* of you?

No one starts their life's journey wanting to be mediocre. Whatever you choose for your career, your hobbies, and your family, you don't want adequate—you want outstanding. At the end of my life, I want to be known as a person of integrity and character who did the right thing more often than not. I want to be known as a kind person who encouraged others every chance I got. I want people to think I'm funny and humble and not afraid to put myself out there for the world to see.

Do you know what brings each of those things to life?

Crucible moments.

Opportunities to fail and fall and make mistakes. The things that I fear have the power to shape me.

The things that you fear have the power to shape you. Never waste an opportunity to grow. It's those tough moments that drive us to greatness.

A Choice to Make

The question is, what will you do with your fears?

Will they be a heavy burden that you shoulder each day? Will they be one more *Soulcrusher* that keeps you from being the you you were meant to be? Or will you let these words give you a shakedown that changes your perspective of your fears and robs them of some of their power?

I hope you choose that. It's liberating to your soul and provides you with a way to live life as you should. Authentically you.

REPLACING FEAR WITH SOMETHING BETTER

This exercise below will help you move from fear to confidence. Think about the fears you are struggling with and use the five steps below to release the weight your fears are pressing on your soul.

Acknowledge:

I struggle with fear. Each day I pick up my fears of __________________________. This is a choice that I make in the morning. No one forces it on me; it is my choice.

Decide:

I will face moments today when I will struggle with the fear of ____________________. When this happens, I will have to decide what to do. I can either give in to that fear and allow it to control me, or I can refuse to allow that fear to have any power over me.

Deflect/Defer:

Instead of choosing to be or feel afraid, I will choose to be confident. I will remember that God has redeemed me and called me by name. His hand guides my steps and His power guards over me. His promises are mine. He has given me talents, skills, and abilities that are unique to me. I may go through difficult times, but I won't go through them alone.

Reflect:

Today, I struggled with ____________________

____

____*. In spite of my struggle, I survived. I was able to do what I needed to do. Tomorrow, I will be prepared for this same struggle. I won't let it control me, and I won't let it have as much power as it did today.*

Anticipate:

Tomorrow, I will likely struggle with ________

____

again. I accept this and reaffirm that it is my choice as to how I react to this struggle. I can pick up that burden again, or I can cast it off and relieve it of its power over me. I will not give it that power; it has no place in my life. I will call upon the mighty power of God to protect me and deliver me through whatever tomorrow brings.

ACTION STEPS

1. **RATE** your level of fear on a scale of 1 to 10. How often does it affect you?

2. **THINK** about the authentic you. How does fear keep you from being who God made you to be? What might happen if you had the courage to simply be yourself?

3. **WRITE** down a list of the fears that constantly bother you. Out to the side of each item on your list, write what you can control and what you can't. Spend some time working on controlling what you can and letting go of what you can't.

4. **THINK** about your strengths and gifts. Write down a statement that describes you in light of your gifts. For example, I might write that *I have been lovingly created by God for just this moment in history. He's given me the ability to see the best in others, encourage them with my words, and help them live their best story. I am a loving husband, a gentle father, a hard worker, and a loyal friend.* Use your statement to shout truth to your fears and refine your authenticity.

5. **COMPLETE** the affirmations above.

QUOTES

To Help You Fragment Fear

"Fear not, for I have redeemed you; I have called you by name, you are mine."

ISAIAH 43:1

"Inaction breeds doubt and fear. Action breeds confidence and courage. If you want to conquer fear, do not sit home and think about it. Go out and get busy."

DALE CARNEGIE

"I learned that courage was not the absence of fear, but the triumph over it. The brave man is not he who does not feel afraid, but he who conquers that fear."

NELSON MANDELA

"He who has overcome his fears will truly be free."

ARISTOTLE

"Keep your fears to yourself, but share your courage with others."

ROBERT LOUIS STEVENSON

2

DESTROY DOUBT

OUR DOUBTS ARE TRAITORS, AND MAKE US LOSE THE GOOD WE OFT MIGHT WIN, BY FEARING TO ATTEMPT.

William Shakespeare,
Measure for Measure

Doubting Thomas. Even if you aren't familiar with the Bible, you've probably heard the name. Thomas was one of Jesus' original twelve disciples. On the night of his arrest, Jesus' disciples fled, scattering to safety. Over the weekend that followed, they watched as this man who fed thousands out of seemingly nothing, caused storms to still with just a word from his mouth, and brought the dead back to life seemed to lose all his power.

They watched Jesus beaten, mocked, and ultimately violently killed.

So three days later, when Thomas got word that Jesus had come back to life, he was skeptical. He doubted, earning a nickname that would persist for centuries. Thomas said, "Unless I see the nail marks in his hands and put my finger where the nails were, and put my hand into his side, I will not believe." For Thomas, just *hearing* Jesus was alive was not enough. He needed proof.

Jesus came to Thomas and gave him the proof he required, allowing Thomas to see and feel the wounds and look into the eyes that he knew so well: He said to Thomas, "Put your finger here; see my hands. Reach out your hand and put it into my side. Stop doubting and believe."

Is Doubt So Bad?

To be honest, I've always thought that Thomas gets a bit of a bad rap.

Post-traumatic stress disorder hadn't been invented yet, but there can't be many more things in life more stressful than the events leading up to that first Easter Sunday. It's understandable that Thomas would doubt that Jesus came back to life, even knowing what he knew and had witnessed and heard from Jesus himself.

Thomas was not thinking clearly, and that's the problem with doubt. It causes us to question what we know to be true and replace it with a lie that is false. It turns our eyes and our focus from what is sound and distracts them with what is shaky. Doubt is insidious because it affects relationships with those we are closest to and pushes us to a kind of self-imposed isolation that is a fertile ground for the seeds of doubt to grow unchecked.

The Thorny Seeds of Doubt

The worst part of doubt is that it feels right at the time. Think about it for a moment. Where does doubt start? Isn't it usually from a lie that feels true? See if any of these sound familiar:

- No one could ever love someone like me.
- I'll never be able to measure up to my parents' standards.
- Why would God want to forgive me after what I've done?
- I'll never be as good as the other players on the team.
- I'll never be a *real* writer/singer/artist.
- Sure he/she said ______, but they really meant ______.
- I'll believe it when I see it.
- I've heard it all before.

These small seeds of doubt are like the first salvos of an attack. These small bricks stack up one by one to form the foundation of a wall that doubt uses to surround your soul. Brick by brick, doubt causes you to wall your heart off from the people closest to you. These small seeds drive deep roots into the crevasses in your heart and lodge there, unwilling to let go.

Doubt feels good at first because it's something you control that takes away the pain of insecurity. It's also an excuse that many people use to keep from taking accountability for their lives. But don't get too comfortable with doubt—it has a very dark side.

THE DOWNSIDE OF DOUBT

Doubt may feel right at first, but ultimately it becomes a Soulcrusher. It snuffs out the good in your life and pulls you to a dark place of distrust. It's like a herd of lions that separates an old, young, or weak member of the herd and devours it.

Doubt Can Crush Your Self-Esteem

When I was a kid, I can remember creating an "IALAC tag" in elementary school. I don't remember the grade, but a counselor had us cut out a piece of construction paper into a rectangle. We used a hole punch to create two holes in the upper right and left corners. Then she had us tie a piece of yarn to each corner so we could hang the rectangle around our neck like a necklace. On the construction paper, she had us glue in big, die-cut, capital letters—I.A.L.A.C. The letters formed an acronym that stood for *I Am Lovable and Capable.*

It's funny how things like that stick in your head thirty-five years later.

The point of the exercise was to provide a tangible way to let kids know that they are *worth loving* and *able to do the big things* they hoped to do one day. I think more kids could use this message today. The interesting part was what happened after we made the tags. The counselor told us that if we said something unkind or hurtful to a classmate, we tore a piece of their IALAC tag off. Tear enough pieces off, and there won't be anything left.

In this social media-saturated world, we could use a reminder like this.

Doubt is a Soulcrusher because it works on you from the inside. If a particular person tears you down, you can usually walk away and get around different people who build you up. But doubt is insidious. It tells you you aren't lovable or capable at a frequency that *only you can hear.* It's the damaging self-talk that you can never get away from. The results can be devastating to your self-esteem and cause you to constantly compare yourself to everyone else. (Who, by the way, are dealing with their own doubts, no matter how good they look on the outside.)

This comparison trap is a slippery slope that doubt loves to throw at you because it takes your focus off the truth and puts it on a lie. Let me remind you right here and right now: you are lovable (even when you are grouchy, tired, mean, and ornery) and capable (even when you don't feel like or are worried about your capabilities).

Don't let doubt tell you otherwise.

Doubt Can Steal Your Confidence

There's something called *impostor syndrome* that most people deal with on a daily basis. Basically, it's a fear that you don't belong, that you're not good enough, or experienced enough, or worth listening to. It's the feeling that other people are more talented, more qualified, or better suited to a task or situation. This is another way that doubt manifests itself.

It doesn't matter your age, your education, your experience, or your qualifications. It affects teachers, preachers, parents, children, successes, failures, and anyone in between. Impostor syndrome is a symptom of the doubt that steals your confidence and causes you to forget what you know and believe a lie. It whispers in your ear that you will fail, that people will laugh, that you don't belong, and you don't deserve the good things that come your way. You can credit this to doubt. It's just another way that doubt tries to derail you and crush you and pull you off the path that only you were meant to take.

Could you stumble if you tried? Of course. But only you know how much time and effort and work you put in to get to the place you are. No one else can take that away from you. Not even doubt.

Doubt Robs You of Your Ability to Trust

Why is it that you don't trust a person? Usually, it's because you doubt their intentions or their word. It could be that they've given you reason in the past, or it could just be that you are unwilling to give them the chance to do so in the future. Either way, doubt can rob you of your ability to trust. It makes you paranoid about others' intentions because it's a reflection of your own insecurities and fears.

If you go through life unable to trust people, especially those closest to you, you wall yourself off from deep relationships and create a sort of self-imposed prison. Doubt knows this. It wants you cut off and unwilling to trust because there it speaks lies into your mind and convinces you that it was right all along.

Doubt Can Cause You to Lose Focus

I'm a huge fan of the Indiana Jones movies. From the fedora to the whip to the sarcastic comebacks, Indiana Jones is a cool character. The third movie, *Indiana Jones and the Last Crusade,* is my favorite. It's got a bumbling Sean Connery as Indy's father, and their interactions as father and son are fantastic.

At the end of the movie, there's a scene inside the temple carved out of the rock at Petra in Jordan. Indy is after the Holy Grail, the legendary cup of Christ that Jesus used at the Last Supper. Indy's dad has spent his whole life researching the final resting place of this cup and uncovering the traps and challenges a searcher will face in finding it.

One of the final challenges Indy must face is a walk across a bridge of faith. Standing on the edge of a chasm that appears infinite, he must step out in faith to reach the other side. If he doubts, he falls to his death.

No big deal, right?

Doubt can be like that for us. It can cause you to lose focus and make small things big and big things impossible. Losing focus comes when you remove your eyes from the truth. Remember at the start of this chapter I said that doubt causes us to remove our eyes from that which is sound and place them on something that is shaky. If you want to move forward, you've got to stay resolute and refuse to let doubt shift your focus.

CRUSHING DOUBT

Doubt can be paralyzing, but it doesn't have to be debilitating. Like anything with power, it can be controlled and actually used for good. The key is to learn to recognize it for what it is and bend it to your will. Here are some of the ways to use doubt to your advantage.

Doubt Can Cause You to Examine Your Beliefs and Clarify What You Think

When (Doubting) Thomas touched the scars in Jesus' side and hands, what do you think happened to his doubt? It probably took off faster than a Texas tornado. Similarly, when Peter denied Jesus three times, he probably doubted everything he'd learned about Jesus and about himself in the past three years of Jesus' ministry. When he heard that Jesus was alive, he probably doubted that Jesus would even look at him, much less love him. But when Peter talked with Jesus on the shore, his doubts were gone when the Word of Truth spoke truth.

Doubt can be good because it forces you to examine what you believe and decide whether it's worth living and maybe even dying for. Far too many people simply believe something just because someone told them to or it was the majority opinion. They haven't actually taken the time to figure out what they think. This is dangerous in life and especially dangerous in faith.

Doubting forces you to examine what you think, consider the facts and evidence, and make a reasoned judgment. This is critical because it shapes your worldview, how you live your life, your values and principles, and the very code you live by. Doubt can refine these things until the impurities are removed and you are left with a distilled and pure faith that is the keystone of all that you are.

Doubt Can Be a Catalyst for Growth

Perhaps it's just the twelve-year-old boy in me, but I never want to be told I can't do something. It's like a personal challenge that I have to overcome. Climb that rock? You bet I can. Doesn't matter if I'm over forty and have creaky knees and intermittent back problems. I'm not backing down from a challenge.

Doubt—whether directed at your abilities or as part of your internal dialogue—can be a powerful catalyst for growth. Now, to be clear, I'm not talking about doing something stupid that is obviously a bad idea. But I am talking about learning a new skill, a new language, a new job, or a new relationship. We all face a moment of doubt before we try something new. That's what makes it exhilarating. If we didn't face and overcome that doubt, how would we grow?

If you are stuck, and it's been a long time since you've grown, it may be time to face your doubts and see if you can use them to push you on. Doubts don't have to hold you back. They can be the impetus for growth that is just what you need.

Doubt Can Stretch You and Reinforce Your Faith

I want to be careful here when it comes to faith. I don't know if you are a person of faith or not, so I'll give you two different takes on this. There's a difference between having doubts *about your faith* and *doubting God*. When you doubt God, you are demonstrating a *lack of faith* and a lack of belief in his promises. God has proven again and again that he will do what he says: the Bible is filled with stories of proof.

But doubt that causes you to question things you don't understand is good. That kind of doubt causes you to seek wisdom and counsel from people you trust. It causes you not to take things for granted but rather to deepen your faith and grow in wisdom and knowledge.

C.S. Lewis, author, preacher, and skeptic used this process to discover his own faith. Here is what another author wrote in the foreword of Lewis's book, *A Grief Observed:*

> *I am grateful, too, to Lewis for having the courage to yell, to doubt, to kick at God with angry violence. This is a part of healthy grief not often encouraged. It is helpful indeed that C. S. Lewis, who has been such a successful apologist for Christianity, should have the courage to admit doubt about what he has so superbly proclaimed. It gives us permission to admit our own doubts, our own angers and anguishes, and to know that they are part of the soul's growth.*

MADELINE L'ENGLE,

foreword to A Grief Observed, by C.S. Lewis

Did you catch that last part? *The soul's growth.* You were never meant to not grow. Biologically your body grows from the day you are conceived. Your soul should grow too, and that growth process is often painful. Here's a hard paradox: you learn much more from the things that hurt than the things that don't.

Don't let doubt derail you. It can be a tool that pushes your soul to grow, your faith to deepen, your willingness to accept who you are to blossom, and your uniqueness to shine.

Franklin D. Roosevelt said, *"The only limit to our realization of tomorrow will be our doubts of today. Let us move forward with strong and active faith."*

Kick that soul-crushing doubt to the curb; it's time to move forward.

REPLACING DOUBT WITH SOMETHING BETTER

This exercise below may help you move from doubt to courage, assurance, and peace. Think about the doubts you are struggling with and use the five steps below to release the weight of your doubts pressing on your soul.

Acknowledge:

I struggle with doubt. Each day I pick up my doubts of ______________________________. This is a choice that I make in the morning. No one forces it on me; it is my choice.

Decide:

I will face moments today when I will struggle with the doubt of ____________________. When this happens, I will have to decide what to do. I can either give in to that doubt and allow it to cripple me, or I can refuse to allow that doubt to have any power over me.

Deflect/Defer:

Instead of choosing to believe a lie and to doubt, I will choose to be courageous and self-assured. I will remember that God has redeemed me and called me by name. His hand guides my steps, and His power guards over me. His promises are mine. He has given me talents, skills, and abilities that are unique to me. I may go through difficult times, but I won't go through them alone. I can choose to believe the truth that I know in my heart and let go of the doubt that is only in my head.

Reflect:

Today, I struggled with ______________________
______________________________________. In spite of my struggle, I survived. I was able to do what I needed to do. Tomorrow, I will be prepared for this same struggle. I won't let it control me, and I won't let it have as much power as it did today.

Anticipate:

Tomorrow, I will likely struggle with ________
____
____________________ again. I accept this and reaffirm that it is my choice as to how I react to this struggle. I can pick up that burden again, or I can cast it off and relieve it of its power over me. I will not give it that power; it has no place in my life. I will call upon the mighty power of God to protect me and deliver me through whatever tomorrow brings.

ACTION STEPS

1. **RATE** your level of doubt on a scale of 1 to 10. How often does it affect you?

2. **LIST** as many doubts as you can think of here. Brainstorm to just get them out of your head and on paper. The idea here is to see how many doubts are lurking around that you may not even know are there. When you see them listed out, you can make a plan to defeat them one by one.

3. **REMEMBER** who you are. Take a look at your list of doubts and identify at least three that you know are not true. Write a corresponding truth that eliminates the doubt. For example, I may doubt my abilities as a writer, but then I can point to the books I've written to *prove* that doubt is not true.

4. **COMPLETE** the affirmations above.

QUOTES

To Help You Destroy Doubt

"If a man will begin with certainties, he shall end in doubts; but if he will be content to begin with doubts, he shall end in certainties."

FRANCIS BACON

"Doubts are the ants in the pants of faith. They keep it awake and moving."

FREDERICK BUECHNER

"Dubium sapientiae initium. (Doubt is the origin of wisdom.)"

RENÉ DESCARTES

"If you hear a voice within you say you cannot paint, then by all means paint and that voice will be silenced."

VINCENT VAN GOGH

"Doubt kills more dreams than failure ever will."

SUZY KASSEM

3

ANNIHILATE ANGER

ANGER IS AN ACID THAT CAN DO MORE HARM TO THE VESSEL IN WHICH IT IS STORED THAN TO ANYTHING ON WHICH IT IS POURED.

Mark Twain

In 2016, Disney Pixar released a movie called *Inside Out.* It was the story of a girl named Riley who, along with her parents, packed up and moved from her home in Minnesota to San Francisco, California. Riley is an eleven-year-old girl who isn't happy with the move. She's a little scared, a little lonely, and not at all excited about leaving her friends, her hobbies, and her home behind.

On the surface, that isn't a very captivating premise for a movie.

This would probably be the reaction of most kids who had to pack up and leave everything they knew behind. What made the story stand out was the way it was told. The movie's director, Pete Docter, had experienced a similar struggle as a kid when he had to move to a new town. He decided to personify the emotions that live inside of Riley's mind and use them to tell Riley's story. In a way that only Pixar can, the curtain is pulled back, and we see Riley's mind at work.

Joy is a colorful, almost effervescent girl who sparkles and glows and has a positive outlook on life. She runs Riley's life from "Headquarters." Disgust is a put-together green girl who causes mischief whenever she can and generally thinks she can do everything better. Sadness is small and blue with a quiet voice, mousy appearance, and a way of bringing everyone down, especially Joy. Fear is a purple guy with buggy eyes and a long nose. He's tall and skinny and sees danger everywhere he looks. Then there's Anger.

Anger is a character all his own. He's short and squat and red in his natural state. He's wearing slacks and a tie and is all business. But you can see the furnace bubbling constantly underneath his slightly unhinged appearance. You know that if he gets pushed too hard, something bad is going to happen, and he's going to blow.

In the movie, when this happens, the top of Anger's head literally erupts into flames. Like a volcano whose relentless underground, unseen pressure and boiling hot magma can't take anymore and must explode, his anger bursts visually upward, a barely contained jet of unruly flames shooting toward the sky.

Sound relatable?

Cracks in the Surface

Everyone who has ever walked the earth can relate to that feeling of anger. You may not show it quite so visually, but you know the feeling you get right before you erupt. It can start small with disgust or frustration. That's the kindling on your fire. It can build through perceived slights or injustices. That's the bigger logs that stoke the flames. It can come to a catalyst when someone's words hit the right nerve or trigger a long-buried emotion or memory. That's the spark.

Then BOOM.

Your fuse is lit; your emotions are burning, and just like that, anger is out of control.

Small things become big things, and you don't know why. People shrink away from you in fear. You may say things you don't mean. You may say things you mean but never meant to say. Once the dam breaks, there's no holding back. You've taken their crap for too long, and you're not gonna take it anymore.

Because let's be honest for a second. Most of the time our anger isn't because a cause we're invested in was harmed or because you see an injustice in the world. Most of the time our anger comes at a more primitive level than that. It comes because of *them* and *they*. People are the ones that push our anger to the boiling point and make it erupt like Mount Vesuvius.

Anger Feels Good

If we want to be really honest, anger feels *good*. It's a little like letting loose on vacation. Ditch those boring business casual office clothes for something a little more freeing and exciting. Always wanted to try a Hawaiian shirt with parrots surfing the rip curl? Go ahead, no one knows you here. Feeling like a Speedo isn't the worst choice in the world? Let it all hang out. You're on vacation. Thinly-veiled societal rules don't apply.

That's how anger makes us feel. It's like releasing the caged animal that we keep in check...most of the time. We may hold it on a leash, but we feed it regularly with the words, insults, hurts, misunderstandings, and shortcomings of those we encounter regularly. Like dried cedar, these things fuel our fire with a quick-burning snap, crackle, pop.

And since it feels so good, we *look* for opportunities to be offended. Have you noticed that about the world we live in today? As I'm writing this, there was recently a flap about an 18-year-old girl that decided to wear a prom dress based on a traditional Chinese style of dress. On social media, she posted pictures of the evening for the world to see, and one person didn't like the "cultural appropriation" of the dress. It blew up into a big deal. I guess that means when you aren't from a particular culture, you can't use/wear/talk about anything from that culture.

This teenage girl and her prom dress went viral as the world discussed whether she should or should not have worn the dress. Even China weighed in on the issue! (For the record, they approved.) You may have strong opinions on what should or shouldn't be posted online (I do!), but really, shouldn't an about-to-graduate student have more important things to worry about than defending her choice of attire at her prom?

Anger didn't think so. The world needed an opportunity to be offended, and by gosh it took it—hook, line, and sinker. Welcome to anger. It feels so good it's like a drug. The problem is this becomes a self-perpetuating cycle. When you want to be offended, it's easy to see opportunities for offense everywhere you look. After all, most people aren't like *us,* and *they* are the ones that make us angry. You can quite literally, think your offenses into existence.

The sad news is that if you want to be angry, the world will give you plenty of fuel for your fire. People are people, and they can be maddeningly frustrating sometimes. I know; I am one. So are you. But if you want to get rid of this Soulcrusher and find the similarities between *them* and you, there is a way. It just takes some consideration and planning.

THE DOWNSIDE OF ANGER

Anger comes from frustration, and frustration is normal. Things don't always—heck, they don't often—work the way we plan. This can be frustrating, especially if you are a control freak. Like a 30-minute sitcom, we want situations to neatly resolve themselves with a tidy laugh track playing in the background. Life doesn't work that way.

So we get frustrated—with ourselves, with circumstances, with others.

And anger kicks in. The injustice of it all! I was made for more than this! Et cetera. Et cetera.

Don't misunderstand me. Anger does have its place, as I'll show you later in this chapter. It can move you to action to stop an injustice. It can motivate you to make a change in your life. Just like a controlled fire can warm you and give you security and a place to cook your food, anger can do good things.

But before you get there, here are some downsides of anger you need to consider:

Anger is an Emotion that Turns Inward

Without a doubt, the biggest downside of anger is that it's an emotion that turns inward. It may seep outward where other people will notice, but first, it takes you over from the inside out. It's a burden you carry constantly that quite literally crushes your soul.

The worst part: no one notices all the energy you spend on being angry.

Anger is a self-inflicted wound. Imagine tumbling down a flight of stairs, dislocating your shoulder, fracturing your ankle, and landing with one arm cut and bleeding through the glass of the back door. You may be clumsy, but the wounds to the shoulder, ankle, and arm are not your fault. Accidents happen. But what you do from that point is up to you.

Imagine dragging yourself to the couch and sitting there a while to replay your fall over and over again in your mind. You notice that your shoulder hurts and your ankle is at a weird angle, but you don't do anything to make them better. Your cut arm is bleeding on your couch, but you don't do anything to stop the flow. You are content to sit and suffer, and you let whatever happens happen.

What would the outcome be? Best case, your cut would scab over so you wouldn't bleed to death; your broken ankle bones would heal but in a weird way, hobbling your walk for the rest of your life, and your shoulder may pop back in place as you squirm around looking for the remote to turn on your news channel of choice to help you reinforce your deeply-held beliefs about *them.*

All the while, your anger would grow—at your situation, at the unfairness of it all, at people for not stopping you from falling, at yourself for not paying attention, at the builder for not making the stairs softer, at the glass company for making it so flimsy.

A seed of bitterness would be planted and take root in the fertile soil of your anger. If someone came to see you, you'd refuse help and sit there in your misery.

Sound graphic and extreme? It is, but that's how anger works.

Anger turns inward and refuses to get better and go away. Replace falling down the stairs with this: an unkind word someone said to you, a disparaging remark about your appearance, a person who acted in a way other than how you wanted them to, a job you lost, a friend who betrayed you, a spouse who left, or a mistake you made. It doesn't matter the trigger, the effects of the wound are no less horrific than a dislocated shoulder, a broken ankle, or a gashed forearm.

Left untreated, these things can be fatal.

Anger Infects Your Relationships

The next thing to go is relationships. I mean, who wants to be around you all dislocated and broken and bleeding? That's no fun for anyone. And you refuse to get help, so people get tired of talking to you. Anger brings about a great deal of self-denial and blindness. When anger is in control, you can't recognize what's going on in your own life.

Remember, it makes you think *they* and *them* are the problem, certainly not you.

So you retreat even further inward as the once-stable relationships in your life crumble. People who cared about you until it hurt stop caring. It's not healthy to be around you anymore, so people walk away. It happens gradually, but your once-thriving garden of relationships now more closely resembles a dried-up patch of weeds who share your misery and choke out the beautiful flowers.

Anger is a poison that infects relationships. It chokes them out and squeezes the life out of them. You become a wizened piece of dehydrated meat that no one—not even your momma—wants to be around. The crazy thing about anger is that many times your anger at a person is over something they might not even be aware of.

They've moved on; you're still mired in the pain.

Anger Robs You of Joy and Peace

It's hard to be joyful when you are angry. We look for things that support our preconceived notions. Think the world is going to hell in a handbasket? You'll be sure to find headlines of murder, assault, and evil. Now there's even a term for it: *doomscrolling.* This is scrolling through the headlines on your phone looking at all the horrible things in the world. What if you think there is some semblance of good in the world? You'll be drawn to stories of a cop who saves a baby's life, a random stranger leaving $100 bills in the grocery store, a person who leaves a huge tip for a waitress who's a single mother, or a child who uses her lemonade stand to raise money for cancer research.

But anger robs you of that joy. It's like wearing Ray Charles' dark glasses over your eyes and then wondering why everything is so gloomy. Everyone else can see the reason but you.

Not only does it rob your joy, but it also steals your peace. Anger is a turbulent storm that leaves your soul at unrest. You don't sleep well; your food doesn't taste good, and you don't find enjoyment in the little things you used to. You're too busy feeling the pain in your dislocated shoulder, or looking at how crooked your ankle looks, or wondering if the cut on your arm is ever going to stop bleeding.

It's hard to have peace when you are constantly battling your wounds.

Anger Causes You to Make Assumptions

I recently heard Bob Goff, author of *Love Does* and *Everybody, Always* speak. If you don't know Bob, you should pick up his books and follow him on social media. He's the fun, crazy uncle that you want to hang out with.

When he was speaking, he gave three basic rules for life when it comes to dealing with others and showing them love. First, he said to *assume that they are smarter than you.* Second, he suggested that you *assume they love God more than you.* And third, he said to ask yourself, *"What's the least creepy explanation for their bad behavior?"*

I'm sure you've noticed that we live in a banged-up, broken world with countless banged-up, broken people. As a result, bad behavior is everywhere. Even the kindest, gentlest person in the world is going to have an off day every so often.

When you are filled with anger, you don't give people the benefit of the doubt, and anger causes you to make assumptions. You see them through your Ray Charles dark glasses and assume the worst. I went to a marriage conference one time, and one of the speakers made a statement I'll never forget. He said, "Bad behavior is a result of pain or a wound that's been left untreated."

Those words have stuck with me as I see broken and wounded people in the world. I think about their lives and what they've gone through to make them the way they are.

It's not easy to love difficult people, but it's downright impossible to love people if you are consumed with anger. You cannot help but see them as a source of your suffering instead of as broken people dealing with suffering of their own.

So on and on the spiral swirls. Anger turns inward, relationships suffer, joy and peace die, and you make unhealthy assumptions of others, which turns anger inward, causing relationships to suffer, joy and peace leak from your soul, and you make unhealthy assumptions of others.

And the beat goes on and on and on...

CRUSHING ANGER

Ironically, once you decide enough is enough, and you are sick and tired of being sick and tired, your anger can become one of the greatest tools to get you back on track and remove that Soulcrusher for good.

It's true. Think about how powerful anger must be if it can keep you pinned to the couch with a dislocated shoulder, broken ankle, and gashed arm. If you can use that power to turn the tide, you can get rid of anger once and for all and develop a system to rid yourself of its hold over you.

Here are some of the ways to channel anger for good:

Anger Over the Right Things Shows Conviction

There's a well-known story of Jesus getting angry in the Temple. He was so angry at what he saw, he paused to make a whip of leather cords to drive the money changers out of the Temple courtyard. What he saw was an affront to God's house, and he was so disgusted he decided to do something about it.

If the Son of God got angry, doesn't that mean that we can too?

There are things in this world that *should* make you angry: social injustice, racism, cruelty, bullying, child abuse, crime, and many, many more. Some of the greatest reformers the world has ever seen have been angry at what they saw. They felt a stirring in their soul that prompted them to make a difference.

Anger can cause you to stand up for something in a way that stiffens your spine and strengthens your resolve. There's a scene in the Marvel movie, *Captain America: The First Avenger,* where Loki (the bad guy) surrounds a group of people outside of a Berlin museum and demands that they kneel before him. As the entire crowd shrinks to their knees, one old man stands up. He says, "I will never again bow to men like you."

It's just a movie, but the message is still powerful. There is certainly evil in the world that should make you angry and cause a reaction. As Edmund Burke said, "The only thing necessary for the triumph of evil is for good men to do nothing." There is a time and place for your anger to inflame and your desire for righteousness to engage.

Anger Forces Self-Evaluation

Once the pity-party ends and you pop your shoulder back into place (Mel Gibson *Lethal Weapon* style), you can start to get over yourself and get to work. Anger, used properly, forces self-evaluation. It makes you ask questions like:

- *Why do I feel like this?* It's okay to feel your feelings. They are real, legit, and true at the time. But asking why you feel like you do helps you pinpoint triggers and determine if those feelings are something that help or harm.
- *What can I do to change?* You'll never get off the couch if you refuse to change. Getting angry about the right things forces you to look at your situation from a new perspective. Often the first step is the scariest, but there are things you can do to change and improve your situation. It may be getting rid of the sweets in your pantry, cutting up your credit card, or reaching out to a concerned friend. Whatever it is, take the first step, and the next one is sure to be easier.
- *What can I add more of to my life? What can I take away?* Life is a series of plusses and minuses. We add and subtract all the time. When you are angry or burdened by other Soulcrushers you take away the good and add the bad. Get angry enough at your circumstances and flip

the equation. Find more good things to add to your life—habits, relationships, actions—and watch things begin to improve.

Once you evaluate your triggers, you can begin to remove the inputs that make you angry. It may mean that you have to stop watching, listening to, or following someone on TV or social media. It may mean that you have to change your surroundings. It may mean that you have to dissolve some toxic relationships. Whatever it takes, if you know certain things make you angry, get serious about getting them out of your life.

Anger Pushes You to Action

There's a point we all reach where we've had enough. We're not gonna take it, no we ain't gonna take it; we're not gonna take it anymore! (If you sang that, we could be friends.) Until you get good and mad about your situation, your life, or your circumstances, you aren't going to change. It's easier to sit on the couch, all dislocated and fractured and gashed, and bemoan the way things are.

But when you finally reach that point where you've had enough, enough of the broken relationships, enough of the dislocated dreams, enough of the gashed hopes, you can finally change. You can finally do something about where you are and make a move toward where you want to be.

It starts when you determine that your future will be different from your present. Anger can push you to action. Instead of being angry at others or angry at circumstances, you can learn to direct your anger at the things you can change. Focused anger pushes you to action. It propels you forward as you decide to demolish everything in your path that stops you from getting where you want to go.

Tired of being fat and sick? Get mad and do something about it. Harness that force that kept you on the couch, and use it to make a change. Sweat. Work. Fight. Tired of being broke? Get mad and do something about it. Change your spending. Make a budget. Visualize a different outcome.

There will always be things you can't control, but there are plenty of things that you can control. Get mad, and get to work on those things. You may just find that some of the things that felt out of control feel a little less challenging and a little more manageable when you defeat anger and put that Soulcrusher to work for you.

REPLACING ANGER WITH SOMETHING BETTER

This exercise below may help you move from anger to action. Think about the things that make you angry that you are struggling with and use the five steps below to release the weight of the anger pressing on your soul.

Acknowledge:

I struggle with anger. Each day I pick up my anger over __________________________________.
This is a choice that I make in the morning. No one forces it on me; it is my choice.

Decide:

I will face moments today when I will struggle with the anger over __________________________.
When this happens, I will have to decide what to do. I can either give in to that anger and allow it to fester, or I can refuse to allow that anger to have any power over me.

Deflect/Defer:

Instead of choosing to be or feel angry, I will choose acceptance. I will remember that God has redeemed me and called me by name. His hand guides my steps, and His power guards over me. His promises are mine. He has given me talents, skills, and abilities that are unique to me. I may go through difficult times, but I won't go through them alone.

Reflect:

Today, I struggled with ______________________
______________________________. *In spite of my struggle, I survived. I was able to do what I needed to do. Tomorrow, I will be prepared for this same struggle. I won't let it control me, and I won't let it have as much power as it did today.*

Anticipate:

Tomorrow, I will likely struggle with ________

____

again. I accept this and reaffirm that it is my choice as to how I react to this struggle. I can pick up that burden again, or I can cast it off and relieve it of its power over me. I will not give it that power; it has no place in my life. I will call upon the mighty power of God to protect me and deliver me through whatever tomorrow brings.

ACTION STEPS

1. **RATE** your level of anger on a scale of 1 to 10. How often does it affect you?

2. **NAME** your emotions. Many times we feel the symptoms of anger but don't recognize the root cause. Take some time to think about the things that you are feeling right now, and consider the root cause. It may be that anger at a person or situation is the root that must be destroyed before anything else can change.

3. **ADD** and take away. Think about the facets of your life and consider what you should add more of and what you should take away. If any facet is causing your anger to rise, it may be time to cut them loose and replace them with something better.

4. **COMPLETE** the affirmations above.

QUOTES

To Help You Annihilate Anger

"Fools give full vent to their rage, but the wise bring calm in the end."

PROVERBS 29:11

"A gentle answer turns away wrath, but a harsh word stirs up anger."

PROVERBS 15:1

"The best fighter is never angry."

LAO TZU

"Anybody can become angry — that is easy, but to be angry with the right person and to the right degree and at the right time and for the right purpose, and in the right way — that is not within everybody's power and is not easy."

ARISTOTLE

"Speak when you are angry and you will make the best speech you will ever regret."

AMBROSE BIERCE

"How much more grievous are the consequences of anger than the causes of it."

MARCUS AURELIUS, MEDITATIONS

"There are two things a person should never be angry at, what they can help, and what they cannot."

PLATO

"Men in rage strike those that wish them best."

WILLIAM SHAKESPEARE, OTHELLO

"Whate'ers begun in anger ends in shame."

BENJAMIN FRANKLIN

4

BOMB bitterness

AS I WALKED OUT THE DOOR TOWARD THE GATE THAT WOULD LEAD TO MY FREEDOM, I KNEW IF I DIDN'T LEAVE MY BITTERNESS AND HATRED BEHIND, I'D STILL BE IN PRISON.

Nelson Mandela

At the time I'm writing this, I have been to Walt Disney World eleven times. The first was when I was eleven or twelve years old and my dad got some free tickets from his work. There's a pretty amazing picture of me wearing my 1980s short shorts and tall, three-stripe Mr. T tube socks pulled up to my knees standing in front of the *Welcome to Florida!* sign with my parents and little sister to mark the occasion.

The second time I went was with my aunt and uncle. They decided to borrow my grandparents' Airstream trailer and camp in Disney's Fort Wilderness campground for a week. I'm not sure what they were thinking—they were used to living in a giant house with lots of space, so being crammed in a sardine can for a week was a little trying. By the last day, my uncle couldn't take it anymore and sprung for a thousand-dollar-a-night room at the Swan and Dolphin Resort.

Years went by, and I got married, started my own family, and finally saved enough money to go back to see Mickey. Our first trip was in 2009. We went back in 2012, again in 2014 with my niece and nephew, and then every year since then. Yes, it can be expensive. Yes, it can be crowded. But the memories we've made there are worth every penny. It's not called the Happiest Place on Earth for nothing.

If you go to EPCOT, you'll find a little shop tucked around a corner called Club Cool. It's a great place to duck into the air conditioning on a hot Florida day. Club Cool is a partnership with Coca-Cola, and they have several stations set up where you can try out beverages from around the world. They provide small cups, and you can get a squirt of Krest Ginger Ale from Mozambique, Fanta Kolita from Costa Rica, Beverly from Italy, Vegeta Beta from Japan, Kinley Lemon from

Israel, Lift Apple from Mexico, Smart Watermelon from China, or Mezzo Mix from Germany.

If you are used to the syrupy sweet soda flavors that the United States has to offer, your taste buds are in for an adventure. But the flavor that gets the strongest reaction, hands down, is Beverly. It's a little bit of an inside joke to suggest to newcomers that they "try the Beverly next" and then watch their faces as they take the first sip.

You see Beverly is notoriously bitter.

It's nothing like a bubbly, fizzy, sweet, ice-cold, we've-been-doing-it-this-way-since-1886 glass of Coca-Cola. It's more like pulling a cactus root (do cacti have roots?) from the ground, boiling it in water, and drinking whatever it creates. (Sorry Italians, I'm big on pasta, not so much on Beverly.)

On our most recent trip, we all took a slug of Beverly and shot video of the strange transformations our faces took when it hit our first bitter taste buds. We were not disappointed. It's even better in slow motion.

THE DOWNSIDE OF BITTERNESS

Bitterness is like nothing else in the world. As a taste, you may not be able to explain it to somebody in words, but you sure know what it is when you get some in your mouth. It's like that in life too, except everyone knows what a bitter person looks, acts, and behaves like. Except, ironically, that person. Often a person who is racked with bitterness is blinded to their condition. They go along, beautiful faces screwed up, twisted into ugly grimaces that a glass of Beverly could learn a thing or two from.

Defining Bitterness

It's taken me about four months to type this sentence. I cranked out the chapters on fear, doubt, and anger. It was easy to describe those feelings and emotions. It was also easy to talk about the upside of those things. As I explained, there are some positive things to come out of fear, doubt, and anger. But when it comes to bitterness, it's hard to find a silver lining. No one wants to be around a bitter person. I believe people who are bitter don't really want to be bitter. It's as hard to use bitterness as a motivator as it is to use poison as a means for growth. Bitterness represents everything wrong and nothing right. So it took me a while to wrap my head around what to do with this chapter, because honestly, the topic is kind of a downer.

But in a way that makes sense doesn't it?

If you've felt the icy cold tentacles of bitterness encircling your heart, you know what I mean. It's what I imagine sinking into quicksand would feel like. You know you're in a bad place; you feel its constricting vice grabbing ahold of you; you start to struggle and resist, but that only seems to make it worse, and eventually, you sink into the mire and remain stuck until it destroys you.

Sounds dramatic, right? I assure you that bitterness is that serious. So if there's no real upside to bitterness, that means we've got to get better at recognizing why it exists and how to resist it before it draws us in. Let's start with a few assumptions that will help you cut through the tangle of bitterness and find clarity.

The World is a Broken Place

Turn on the news, open social media, read the headlines, and what will you find? A running list of all the things wrong with the world. Emotions running high as one person or organization says something that offends another. Hurricanes, tornadoes, earthquakes, floods, war, human trafficking, the opioid epidemic, racial injustice, oppression, abortion, suicide, depression, and famine are just a few of the by-products of a broken world. As I write this, we've been in a global pandemic for months, and we're seeing the aftermath of a never-before-seen messy election.

In his book, *Love and War*, John Eldredge says marriage is, "a love story set in the midst of a war." But the war metaphor goes far beyond relationships. If you are a Christian, you may not see the enemy, but you can recognize his handiwork and know without a doubt he is there.

The wreckage of trashed dreams, broken relationships, death, and destruction lies all around. Is there beauty and wonder and hope there too? Absolutely, but it is found in glimpses and glances with a broken world as its backdrop. It is against this backdrop where we find ourselves trying to rise from the mire.

The Broken World is Filled with Broken People

We may hide it well, but every one of us is broken. We plaster on big smiles and clean up our social media profiles to only show us at our best. When we succeed with anything—getting the job, asking for a date, losing the weight, starting a business—we often gloss over all the difficulty and hard times that got us there. That's why when we find someone who is willing to be transparent and show us the down and dirty behind the scenes, it resonates.

But a broken world filled with broken people is a hard place to exist.

Broken people make poor choices, and those poor choices have sometimes catastrophic consequences. These consequences don't just affect the person making the choice; they affect everyone around them. Like an exploding grenade, the shrapnel flies indiscriminately and strikes whoever's in range. It may be intentional or it may be unintentional, but the damage is done just the same.

It's in these wounds that the infection of bitterness begins to spread.

Instead of seeing broken people and filling with compassion for their hurting hearts, we see people who have let us down, caused us pain, and deserve wrath and retribution. Have you ever bit the side of your mouth and caused a sore spot? What inevitably happens to that wound? You bite it again and again, and it takes forever to heal.

So it is with bitterness.

The first piece of shrapnel that strikes you may come as a terrible surprise. But when the next comes you sort of expect it. Then as more and more shots are fired, you've resigned yourself to the fact that the person who has wounded you is undeserving of love and compassion because they are obviously wounding you on purpose.

The Circumstances of Those Choices are Out of Your Hands

Chuck Swindoll said, "Life is 10% what happens to you and 90% how you react to it." We are at the whim of the circumstances of our lives. When you wake up tomorrow, you will have good things happen to you and bad things happen to you. You may have a flat tire on the way to work, or you may find a $20 bill on the ground in the parking lot. Someone will compliment your shoes or hair, and it will boost your mood.

Someone else will let the door slam in your face, cut you off in traffic, or say something unkind or negative that pricks your heart and causes you pain.

Unless you live alone as a hermit in a cave in the middle of nowhere, you can't do too much to change your circumstances. Of course, you can build a better life, get an education, move to a different city, make new friends, and hang out with different people.

But that's not really the issue, is it?

Because if you're honest with yourself, none of those things are really the problem. The real problem is how you *react* when circumstances don't go your way.

I've had conversations with people who were angry at someone about something. Many times the person who made them angry didn't even know it. But rather than letting that 10% go and reacting with 90% love and grace, they invert the equation. They give 10% love and grace (because you know, Jesus and everything) and nurse that hurt and pain with the other 90% of their efforts. They imagine the person's actions to be worse than they were. They add premeditation and forethought. Like a bandit on the side of the road, they imagine the offender sat in the weeds scheming for ways to get them as they walked by.

Friends, I'm not minimizing your pain. And to be clear, I'm writing this as much to me as I am to you. But when you look at the paragraph above, does anything in there strike a chord in your heart? Just because someone made a comment that hurt you, does it mean that they are your enemy and did it on purpose? Sometimes, maybe, the answer is yes. If that's the kind of person they are, then you need to cut them loose and find different people to be around. But most of the time, it's because they are a broken person in a broken world dealing with all the pain and hurt and sadness that comes with it—just like you.

CRUSHING BITTERNESS

So—broken person in a broken world—you have a choice to make.

You can let the wounds of a stranger or friend fester and turn into bitterness. Or you can see these wounds for what they are—the by-product of *their struggle* through life and an opportunity to love them better and more fully.

I'm not saying this will be easy.

In fact, it will likely be a struggle you have to make up your mind to conquer each and every day. Remember, a Soulcrusher is already in the bag just waiting for you to pick it up each morning and pull it out.

It feels comfortable because it's been with you for so long.

Many days you'll be tempted to pick up that pain of bitterness and savor it for a while. In a strange way, it can become a kind of fuel. But love is better. What if today you put down the bitterness and reacted with love? What if instead of seeing all the things that reinforce your bitterness and prove your point, you worked hard to look for the opposite things? What if instead of seeing malice in another's eyes you saw pain and fear?

How would that change how you reacted? You have a choice to make. We all do. Pick up that burden of bitterness. Wrap its cords around your neck and your heart, and let it squeeze you and bleed you dry. It will hurt at first, but you'll get used to it.

But at what cost?

As damaged relationships fall by the wayside, you'll get by on your own, but it won't be a very full life. You'll think back to what could have been and might have been and should have been if only you'd been a little more patient, a little more compassionate, a little more understanding, a little more loving.

You'll be on your island, but that is a lonely place to be.

Or you choose love. You shake loose of the cords of bitterness that bind you. The opposite of bitterness is acceptance. It's seeing people through the eyes of compassion and understanding. It's giving them the benefit of the doubt because you'd hope they would do the same for you. So you make a choice. You choose daily to see the best in people instead of the worst.

You talk about the good times instead of the bad. You see people as just the same as you—broken, hurting, wounded—but trying to get by in this world and do their best. And as a result, the chains of bitterness that weigh you down will begin to fall away.

It will take time and concerted effort on your part, but that's what this book is all about: making the decision to lighten the burden on your soul and breathe the fresh air of freedom. I promise you it will taste incredibly sweet.

REPLACING BITTERNESS WITH SOMETHING BETTER

This exercise below may help you move from bitterness to acceptance. Think about the people who you are holding hostage to bitterness and use the five steps below to release the shackles that are holding them—and you—hostage.

Acknowledge:

I struggle with bitterness. Each day I pick up my bitterness over these situations and these people:
____
______________________________________. *This is a choice that I make in the morning. No one forces it on me; it is my choice.*

Decide:

I will face moments today when I will struggle with the bitterness over _______________________. When this happens I will have to decide what to do. I can either give in to that bitterness and allow it to fester, or I can refuse to allow that bitterness to have any power over me.

Deflect/Defer:

Instead of choosing to be or feel bitter, I will choose acceptance. I accept the people in my life as broken and hurting—just like me. I will remember that God has redeemed me and called me by name. His hand guides my steps, and His power guards over me. His promises are mine. He has given me talents, skills, and abilities that are unique to me. I may go through difficult times, but I won't go through them alone. Today I will love the people in my life in spite of anything they do or say that hurts me.

Reflect:

Today, I struggled with ____________________. In spite of my struggle, I survived. I was able to do what I needed to do. Tomorrow, I will be prepared for this same struggle. I won't let it control me, and I won't let it have as much power as it did today.

Anticipate:

Tomorrow, I will likely struggle with ____________ ____ ________________________ again. I accept this and reaffirm that it is my choice as to how I react to this struggle. I can pick up that burden again, or I can cast it off and relieve it of its power over me. I will not give it that power; it has no place in my life. I will call upon the mighty power of God to protect me and deliver me through whatever tomorrow brings.

ACTION STEPS:

1. **RATE** your level of bitterness on a scale of 1 to 10. How often does it affect you?
2. **LIST** all the people or circumstances that are causing you to be bitter. Don't hold back; be honest with yourself and write down everything you think of.
3. **THINK** about your feelings. What is there in your heart that allows this to be a source of pain?
4. **CONSIDER** their feelings. What difficulties or struggles are they facing that could have led to their words or actions?
5. **BEGIN** to pray daily over these people or circumstances and ask God to release the grip of bitterness that imprisons you. In time you may feel the need to reach out to the person and ask their forgiveness.
6. **COMPLETE** the affirmations above.

QUOTES

To Bomb Bitterness

"Bitterness is like cancer. It eats upon the host."

MAYA ANGELOU

"As we pour out our bitterness, God pours in his peace."

F.B. MEYER

"Bitterness is like drinking rat poison and waiting for the rat to die."

JOHN ORTBERG, JR.

"There's no such thing as a bitter person who keeps the bitterness to himself."

ERWIN W. LUTZER

"Never trust your tongue when your heart is bitter."

SAMUEL J. HURWITT

"There is only one way of victory over the bitterness and rage that comes naturally to us—to will what God wills brings peace."

AMY CARMICHAEL

"When the root is bitterness, imagine what the fruit might be."

WOODROW KROLL

"Frequently the enemy entices Christians to harbor an unforgiving spirit—a very common symptom indeed among God's children. Such bitterness and fault-finding and enmity inflict a severe blow upon spiritual life."

WATCHMAN NEE

"That which is bitter to endure may be sweet to remember."

THOMAS FULLER

"Bitterness imprisons life; love releases it."

HARRY EMERSON FOSDICK

5

WIPE OUT WORRY

WORRY GIVES A SMALL THING A BIG SHADOW.

Swedish Proverb

Imagine for a minute that all your mental capacity is like the processor in your computer.

On a computer, every browser tab you open takes processing power. Every program you open takes processing power. When you watch a video, it takes processing power. When you play music, it takes processing power. No matter how much memory your computer has, at some point, it will reach its limits. If it's like the nine-year-old Macbook I'm typing on now, when you reach your limits, the cursor arrow turns into "the beachball of death"—a colorful spinning circle that reminds me that I tried to do too much at once, and now I'm paying the price.

I do a lot of video calls for my work, and when I get on one of these calls, it eats up the memory on my computer. The fan starts whirring incessantly; the computer gets hot to the touch, and I have to start closing down things I'm not using.

Another example is your battery usage on your phone. Go to your settings and click battery usage, and it will give you a breakdown of what's draining your battery. You'll probably be surprised at some of the things that are running in the background and chewing away at your capacity. Shut them down, and you immediately free up space and energy.

What goes on in your mind works in much the same way. All your thoughts, ideas, and worries take up valuable mental space. This is especially true of worry. It's like that program that's running in the background all the time, draining you of your energy, and you don't know why.

Worry is a devious little Soulcrusher because it's just kind of there. It's like a constant ache or continual pressure with no clear specific source. It's just a thing you wake up with and go to sleep with and hope that one day will leave you alone. Yet when you are a worrier, it never does.

THE DOWNSIDE OF WORRY

Author Max Lucado once wrote, "Worry divides the mind." If you've worried at all about anything ever (and who hasn't?), you likely know the truth of this statement. When you have a worry, it's constantly at the forefront of your thoughts. You can do things to take your mind off your worry, but like a boomerang, it comes flying back. My wife put it this way, "At night when things are the quietest is when my worries are the loudest."

Even worse though is the fact that worry divides your attention and energy from the important things and places it on the things that may never happen. It's a devious little system that keeps you from getting the important things done. As the worries go up, this division multiplies exponentially. The quicker you can get a handle on your worries, first by recognizing what they are and what they are not, the quicker you can lighten your load and move forward with peace.

Worry Gives a Small Thing a Big Shadow

Is there a more appropriate description of worry? Worry is a master of deception. Have you ever made the mistake of Googling a health problem? You know, when you have a rash or a dull pain or a nagging cough, so you take it to the internet to see what Dr. Google says it could be. The rash could be the start of shingles, which has been known to knock down even the healthiest of individuals. The dull pain is probably the start of a degenerative bone disease that will leave you unable to get out the bed.

And the cough, don't even get me started on the cough. Chances are, it's from a rare bug you picked up because you didn't wash your vegetables.

The end is near friends. Time to say goodbye.

Or maybe the rash is just poison ivy that you picked up from working in the yard. The dull pain is because you're a little clumsy in the mornings before you've had caffeine, and you bumped into the coffee table. And the nagging cough is because you stirred up dust when you ran the vacuum.

This is how worry works.

It takes a small concern, turns it into a nagging thought in your mind, and blows it way out of proportion. As Mark Twain humorously said, "I am an old man and have known a great many troubles, but most of them have never happened."

Worry Zaps Your Energy

The older I get, the more I value the energy I expend. It comes from wisdom, I suppose. When you are young, the days stretch on forever, and you try new things and often race around chasing anything that comes your way. When you get older, you become more discerning with how and where you spend your time.

Quite frankly, worry is a lot of work.

It chews up mental capacity. It zaps your energy as you vividly imagine all of the worst-case scenarios and their possible outcomes.

My dad and I used to joke about our "Work Down from Death" method of dealing with worry. We figured that death was the very worst thing that could happen. (Relax believers, I'm not talking about what happens to you when you die, just that when you're gone, you're gone, and your worries don't matter anymore.) As long as I'm still kicking, I can come up with a plan, work through problems, and fight another day. After death came an IRS audit. That's never fun for anyone, probably not even the IRS. Then came sickness, money problems, and other worries. The point is that worrying takes up a lot of mental energy for things that rarely, if ever, happen. That energy is something that would be much better spent elsewhere. Working backward helps you shine some much-needed perspective on the severity of the things you are worrying about.

Worry Assumes Facts Not in Evidence

My dad loved reading the Perry Mason books by Erle Stanley Gardner. These short paperback books followed the famous defense attorney through case after case where he defended the innocent while rooting out the guilty. Later, the Perry Mason TV show featured Raymond Burr as the baritone-voiced attorney. I can remember listening to the show and hearing this line:

"Objection! Assumes facts not in evidence." In law, this means something is presented as true when there has been no evidence to back it up.

If worry were a prosecuting attorney, one of its favorite tactics would assume facts not in evidence. I'm naturally a pretty optimistic person. No matter how stressful things are, I'm usually able to go to sleep, figuring if I get some rest, I can tackle my problems in the morning with a fresh perspective. So I also tend to swing a little too far to the positive side of things. I'm sure I drive my family crazy because if they are negative about something, I'll overcompensate with the positive.

My daughter is just wrapping up her first year of college in the midst of a pandemic, and she's firmly embedded in the "what-if?" part of life. *What if I transfer to the wrong school? What if I make bad grades? What if I don't make any friends? What if I choose the wrong major? What if? What if? What if?*

I'm not downplaying her emotions at all, but it's easy to assume facts not in evidence.

I usually respond with the opposite of her questions. What if you choose the best school for you? What if you flourish and you make the best grades of your life because it's a subject you enjoy? What if you make a lifelong friend or meet the love of your life? No one sticks with their first choice of major.

Worry can crush you with its endless doomsday scenarios and what-ifs.

What if we didn't let that happen?

What if we decided to err on the side of positive and take a wait-and-see approach. I'm not saying it's easy, because I know it's not. But I am saying that it's a vital part of removing this Soulcrusher and living a fully-vibrant life.

CRUSHING WORRY

As frustrating as worry can be sometimes, it does have a place in your life in managed doses. If you never worried about anything, you wouldn't be human. Worry comes because you have hopes and dreams and plans, and you want to make sure those happen. That's a good thing. The world needs more people who work hard to achieve their dreams and make a difference. But like most things, moderation is key. Without it, you'll end up a basket-case paralyzed by indecision and unable to move forward. So here are a few ways to manage worry and the benefits they provide.

Planning Eliminates Worry

When I was a kid growing up, money seemed to always be tight. I'm not sure if it's because my dad was a self-employed carpenter who sometimes struggled to find work, or if it's because he spent a little too freely. But whatever it was, I internalized that money was a huge cause of stress.

It's interesting how a belief formed early on can stick with you for life.

For most of my adult life, I've had a nagging feeling in the back of my mind about money. It's probably my number-one cause of worry. This is ironic because even though we've struggled financially sometimes, we've never missed a meal, and we've been able to be generous with our charitable giving. But that nagging worry still persists.

Your worry may not be money; it may be something else, but this fact remains: when you make a solid plan, you eliminate—or at least drastically minimize—worry. Consider money. You worry because you don't have enough money in the bank account. So how do you combat that? With planning. If you have a job and are careful with your paycheck, live within your means, and make a budget, it drastically cuts down on worry.

When I was teaching in an at-risk youth program, one of the first life-lessons we taught was how to create and stick with a budget. It's amazing how this one little thing can minimize your worry. You don't have to wonder if the money is there if it's in your budget.

But what if, as my wife asked me, you're a mom? How do you minimize *that* worry? As I was thinking about this chapter on worry, my wife made a good point. She *always* worries about our kids. It's something about being a mom. But (at least in my man brain) I think the same point holds true. As parents, we make a plan for our kids and do all we can to prepare them to go out into the world. We tell them to look both ways before crossing the street, don't talk to strangers, always say your prayers, nothing good happens after midnight, and a host of other life lessons.

Then we send them on their way and hope some of the lessons stick.

Proverbs 22:6 says, "Start children off on the way they should go, and even when they are old they will not turn from it." The image here is that of a well-worn path or trail. As a parent, you are embedding those lessons into your children's minds from the day they are born. Each one firms up the path and makes striking off on your own through the woods less appealing. Children will always make mistakes and choices parents don't understand (you did it too), but when you train them up, you can send them out into the world knowing that somewhere inside their minds those lessons are still there.

We can either choose to plan and prepare for what we think will happen and then let it go, or we can worry about every eventuality no matter how unlikely it is. Either way, we really don't know what is going to happen, and we have to move forward in faith.

Worry Unlocks the Shackles of Control

Here's a thought: worry is really just an *illusion* of control.

Think about it.

You worry because you think you can control the outcome. Consider my illustration above. You can plan and budget and prepare for everything you can think of, but if your house burns to the ground or your car dies, it's going to be an inconvenience at best or a catastrophe at worst. We worry because we think we are in control. I don't know if this is a uniquely American thing or if it happens in other cultures, but here's a secret—you aren't in control. None of us are.

Think about your heart. Do you consciously cause it to beat?

Thump-thump. Thump-thump. Thump-thump.

Nope. All on its own, it keeps beating until you take your last breath.

How about your brain waves? Can you control the electrical impulses that keep your body functioning? Nope. That happens on its own too, thanks to the miracle of God's creation. It's the same thing with breathing. Of course you can hold your breath and stop breathing for a time, but at night when you're asleep, you breathe in and out automatically.

Worry fools us into thinking we are in control.

Discovering that you aren't is incredibly freeing because it forces you to put your trust in something else. Again, there's a balance between fatalism and trust. I know that God has a plan for me, and so I do everything in my control to live out my life *in the safety of God's plan.*

You may feel like you don't trust anything but yourself, but really that's a lie. When you enter into a relationship, you give up some of the control of your life and share it with another. When you get a job and have a career, you give up some of your control to your boss or the organization.

Worry or Not, The World Keeps Spinning

If you haven't read this Old Testament wisdom book of Ecclesiastes, you should take a look. It's a fascinating look at life and why much of what we pursue is, as the writer says, "meaningless, meaningless."

In the book, the author (widely considered to be Solomon, the wisest man who ever lived) poses question after question and writes about all the things he's tried to find happiness. Ultimately the world keeps spinning and moving regardless of what we do and what we try.

When it comes to worry, we have a choice. Give in, and imagine all the worst that could happen. Or pause, have faith, and realize that much of what we imagine is only the excess of our minds. It's a spiritual attack that keeps us from the fullness of life God has for us. It's a Soulcrusher whose burden causes untold harm in our lives and our relationships. It's not easy to let this burden that you've carried for so long go, but it is vital to living the life you were meant to live.

REPLACING WORRY WITH SOMETHING BETTER

This exercise below may help you move from worry to trust. Think about the things that constantly cause you to worry, and use the five steps below to release the shackles that are holding you hostage.

Acknowledge:

I struggle with worry. Each day I pick up these worries: ______________________________ ______________________________. This is a choice that I make in the morning. No one forces it on me; it is my choice.

Decide:

I will face moments today when I will struggle with worries about ______________________. When this happens, I will have to decide what to do. I can either give into those worries and allow them to consume my mind, or I can refuse to allow those worries to have any power over me and place my trust in God.

Deflect/Defer:

Instead of choosing to worry, I will choose trust and faith. I accept that there are circumstances beyond my control. I acknowledge that I can choose to act or react to these circumstances. I will remember that God has redeemed me and called me by name. His hand guides my steps, and His power guards over me. His promises are mine. He has given me talents, skills, and abilities that are unique to me. I may go through difficult times, but I won't go through them alone. Today I will trust God's provision, love, and care over me.

Reflect:

Today, I struggled with ______________________ ______________________. In spite of my struggle, I survived. I was able to do what I needed to do. Tomorrow, I will be prepared for this same struggle. I won't let it control me, and I won't let it have as much power as it did today.

Anticipate:

Tomorrow, I will likely struggle with ________________ again. I accept this and reaffirm that it is my choice as to how I react to this struggle. I can pick up that burden again, or I can cast it off and relieve it of its power over me. I will not give it that power; it has no place in my life. I will call upon the mighty power of God to protect me and deliver me through whatever tomorrow brings.

ACTION STEPS

1. **RATE** your level of worry on a scale of 1 to 10. How often does it affect you?
2. **FIND** a quiet place, take some deep breaths, and listen to what's going on in your mind. What worries is it telling you to focus on? List them here.
3. **ON** a scale of 1 to 10, rank the likelihood of any of these worries coming true. After you've done this, order them from most likely to happen to least likely to happen.
4. **START** with the worry that is most likely to come true. What plan can you put in place to minimize the damage? Think about ways you can change the outcome, and write them here. Do this for each worry as you go down the list.
5. **CUT** yourself some slack. Even the best plans will face hiccups and difficulties. Build in a mindset of flexibility and adaptation. When things go wrong, take a step back, regroup, and attack the problem again.

6. **CHANGE** negative self-talk. The voice in your head is powerful. When it starts talking negatively and worry-filled, hit pause, rewind the thought, and spin it to positive. Remember, worry is an imagined worst-case scenario. Be prepared for that scenario to happen, but don't eagerly bring it upon yourself.

7. **COMPLETE** the affirmations above.

QUOTES

To Wipe Out Worry

"Worry does not empty tomorrow of its sorrow; it empties today of its strength."

CORRIE TEN BOOM

"Do not anticipate trouble or worry about what may never happen. Keep in the sunlight."

BENJAMIN FRANKLIN

"Let our advance worrying become advance thinking and planning."

WINSTON CHURCHILL

"How much pain have cost us the evils that have never happened."

THOMAS JEFFERSON

"Therefore do not be anxious about tomorrow, for tomorrow will be anxious for itself. Sufficient for the day is its own trouble."

MATTHEW 6:34 (ESV)

"Never worry alone. When anxiety grabs my mind, it is self-perpetuating. Worrisome thoughts reproduce faster than rabbits, so one of the most powerful ways to stop the spiral of worry is simply to disclose my worry to a friend... The simple act of reassurance from another human being [becomes] a tool of the Spirit to cast out fear—because peace and fear are both contagious."

JOHN ORTBERG

"Worry divides the mind."

MAX LUCADO

"How can a person deal with anxiety? You might try what one fellow did. He worried so much that he decided to hire someone to do his worrying for him. He found a man who agreed to be his hired worrier for a salary of $200,000 per year. After the man accepted the job, his first question to his boss was, "Where are you going to get $200,000 per year?" To which the man responded, "That's your worry."

MAX LUCADO

"Worry is the sin of distrusting the promises and power of God."

CRAIG GROSCHEL

6

UPEND unforgiveness

TO FORGIVE IS TO SET A PRISONER FREE AND DISCOVER THAT THE PRISONER WAS YOU.

Louis B. Smedes

There's a better than average chance you remember this quote: "Get busy living, or get busy dying." If you guessed the movie, *The Shawshank Redemption*, you'd be right. *Shawshank* is one of those kinds of movies that you have to stop to watch when you're channel surfing. It doesn't matter if it's just starting, or if it's the last five minutes. It speaks to so many human emotions that it pulls you in and compels you to watch.

If you haven't seen the movie, which is based on the 1982 Stephen King novella *Rita Hayworth and The Shawshank Redemption*, here's a quick overview. Andy

Dufresne is a banker convicted of murdering his wife and imprisoned at Shawshank Penitentiary.

The only problem: he's innocent.

Andy is mild-mannered and gentle, and he must quickly learn to adapt to prison life under the harsh watch of self-righteous and cruel Warden Samuel Norton. Inside, Andy meets Ellis "Red" Redding, brilliantly played by Morgan Freeman. Red is a contraband smuggler, the "guy who knows how to get things." As the story unfolds and Red and Andy's friendship deepens, Red tells Andy there's only one way to get through prison: "Get busy living, or get busy dying." It's a reminder that we all have a choice no matter what our circumstances may tell us. In the movie, it's a turning point for Andy, who has just about lost hope.

Life Behind Bars

I've never been to prison, so I can only imagine what it's like, especially if you didn't commit the crime of which you were accused. But I do know what it's like to *be* imprisoned. Unfortunately, many of us walk around in a prison of our own making.

Its name: Unforgiveness.

This prison is the cruelest of all because we are both the jailer and the jailed. We hold the key but are all too often unwilling to use it to set ourselves free. We sit in the dark, damp cell and brood. We recall the evidence, replay the trial, and convince ourselves that we are right, we were wronged, and nothing will change our mind.

Then we slam the heavy iron door shut and listen to the satisfying *thunk* of the lock as it reverberates down the halls of our hearts. We unknowingly settle down to do our time and wonder why we are in this dark and lonely place.

Perhaps you think I'm being overly dramatic.

But maybe these words convict because they strike just a little too close to home. Unforgiveness is one of the worst Soulcrushers because it doesn't just stay a burden—it becomes a prison. You might power through fear or doubt, stifle your anger and bitterness, and even overcome worry. But unforgiveness lingers. It's a burden that you carry all on your own, and the reason why is even more devious—because we like it.

Tell me that isn't the truth. If someone has hurt you, maybe grievously, unforgiveness feels justified. It's a defensive maneuver. You did this thing to me, and I had no power to stop it, but what I *do* control is my reaction, so in my heart you are burned, done, finished, the enemy.

I will no longer trust you, love you, nor let you into my life.

I control the situation now.

So you slam the prison door shut, sit on your damp cot with the flimsy mattress, pull the scratchy blanket up to your chin, cross your arms in defiant victory and throw away the key to your life.

Breaking Free

You know this is true because you've felt it—the hurt and betrayal of someone letting you down. They didn't live up to your expectations (expectations, by the way, of which they may not have even been aware), and you lock them out. You think you're raising the drawbridge and closing the gate to shelter inside the safety of your fortress, but really you're locked away, and they are free. This wasn't what you intended for your life. But the longer you hold on to unforgiveness, the rustier and more imposing your prison bars become. Surely, this can't be what's best.

If you want to gain freedom from unforgiveness, you've got to understand what it is and what it isn't. You have to look at your own heart and get honest with yourself. Staying locked away doesn't reduce the pain; it just provides an incubator that causes it to grow unchecked. Unforgiveness is one of those heavy burdens we know we carry in our hearts but don't want to admit. But that's exactly where you must start if you want to break free of its devastating grasp and live the life you were meant to live.

THE DOWNSIDE OF UNFORGIVENESS

I really could skip this paragraph. You probably don't need me to explain all of the bad things that come when you refuse to forgive others. Deep down you know because you've felt them or are feeling them now. At the risk of piling on, let me say this: unforgiveness is laziness. Look, I know life's no picnic, and people hurt you, and it's hard to let that go. But what did you expect? We are broken people living in a broken world. But we are also sanctified people who are commanded to love one another, called to grow closer to Christ, and most of all, *we have been forgiven, ransomed from death, and set free.* How do we have any right to withhold that from others?

The Christian walk is all about process and improvement. It's a continual drive to get better—not because it's the key to our salvation, but because it's what people do when they are in love. And make no mistake, this is about love. The love God has for you and the love He expects you to have for His people. When you are locked in that slimy, dank prison of your unforgiveness, the only love you have is for your own stubbornness and selfishness.

Unforgiveness is an Excuse for Bad Behavior

If you are a parent, you may have spoken the words, "Yes, but that's no excuse for that kind of behavior." We know when we are acting like toddlers even if we are adults. It's no secret what bad behavior looks like. But sometimes we double down because it's embarrassing to admit we were wrong. So we stay on the same path, often acting like a fool, and our bad behavior defines us.

Unforgiveness of others is the ultimate excuse for bad behavior. They (the offender) did this (the offense) to me so I feel hurt (the wound) and therefore I am justified for my (insert bad behavior). This formula can be a treadmill from which there is no escape. Why? There are a few reasons. First, it gives you the illusion of control. You can't control the person, but you can control your reaction to them. So when you close that prison door, you think you are shutting them out, but really you are locking yourself in. Second, there's a perverse pleasure in bad behavior. It's fun to make people suffer when you feel like they deserve it.

Of course, they may not know why you're making them suffer. They may just see someone who is closed off, withdrawn, and angry all the time. Remember, there are at least two sides to everything. By the way, the devil knows that it's fun for you to nurse a grudge and does everything he can to keep you wallowing in the mud.

Finally, let's face it; it's hard to always be the bigger person. To forgive when you don't want to. To let things that hurt you roll off your back. To stay quiet when you feel like shouting. It's against our nature.

We want to stand up, strike back, and level the boom. But who are you listening to when you do that? The old, broken you or the new you who is trying to be more like Christ? It's not easy. I know that. But I don't ever want my bad behavior to drive someone away from me. I'd rather do the hard work of *trying* to be the bigger person, even if I don't always get it right.

Unforgiveness Kills Relationships

Unforgiveness kills relationships. The worst part about that is you were designed for relationships. God didn't need to create Adam and Eve, but He did because He wanted a relationship with them. God didn't need to invent marriage, but He did, because he knew we'd be stronger together and complement each other. God didn't have to send Jesus to die for our sins to restore that broken relationship, but He did because—Love.

When you are locked in that prison of unforgiveness, you aren't just blocking out a relationship with the person who hurt you. You're also shutting out God. Walls are walls, no matter why they are there. It's very difficult for God to pour out His love and forgiveness to you when you are blocked off, hidden, and hunkered down in your cell. He'll still do it; He'll pursue you relentlessly, but it's hard to water a plant that is covered.

You live in a society that is more connected than ever, but loneliness is on the rise. Authentic relationships are hard work because they require vulnerability and trust.

They also require an understanding that even though I may stumble and hurt you, it is not intentional; it doesn't have to define us, and it can be fixed. Too many times, we have a one-strike-and-you're-out policy. We give people one chance to get close, and BOOM, *mess up and you're out of my life.*

Life is tricky enough when we are surrounded by good people who care about us. It's exponentially more difficult when our unforgiveness cuts out relationships one by one. Like a soldier separated from the rest of his unit, it makes us "easy pickin's" for the enemy.

Unforgiveness Isolates You From Those That Love You Most

Have you ever been driving and some inconsiderate, self-absorbed, arrogant jerk cuts you off, squeezes his car in front of your bumper, and then jams on the brakes? Then, when you give him a dirty look, he gives you the one-finger salute in return.

If you're like me when that happens, your heart rate jumps, your pupils dilate, and you immediately tailgate the person to, as my wife says, "show him."

Just kidding, I would never be that immature. But when these situations happen, it's easy to get angry. But how long do you stay angry? I'm sure you can remember an incident where someone cut you off but you've probably let it go by now, right?

That's because that person was a stranger. You didn't know him; you'll never see him again, so you don't waste your energy on staying angry. It's not worth the effort. That's why unforgiveness claims victims who are much closer than that.

Think about it. Who can hurt you the most? The people who are closest to you—friends and family. Strangers come in and out of your life every day. There's no shortage of them. But you only have a select number of friends and family. They can hurt you more because they are closer to you.

When it comes to friends or family, we expect more. They should know better. So when they do something that hurts (again, I would suggest that this is *mostly* unintentional), it stings more than a stranger's wound. Unlike the stranger that took his middle finger and drove away, you have to keep seeing your friends and family, unless you want to end up on Dr. Phil's couch in ten years.

Unforgiveness is a killer because it isolates you from those who really do love you most. They may not always show it, and they may not display it in a way that speaks clearly to you, but they do. So when you allow a wound to fester and unforgiveness to gain a foothold, you isolate yourself from the very people you need in your corner.

Wives and husbands, parents and children, and friends are critical relationships that should shore up and strengthen your walk through life. Unforgiveness knows this and pushes you deeper into your cell and further away from love.

Unforgiveness is a Perpetual Cycle

If you look for something long enough, you will find it. That's what happens with unforgiveness. Once it gains a foothold, it keeps clawing. Pretty soon you'll start to look for other hurts to feel bad about. You'll remember all the other times that person did something to you, and it will reinforce your justification for your behavior. Before long this cycle has devastating effects on other areas of your life. If you get into the habit of unforgiveness, it erodes your ability to trust. You wall yourself off further with the lie that if you don't trust, you can't get hurt. This may be true of external wounds, but what is the cost on your soul if you never trust again?

CRUSHING UNFORGIVENESS

By this point, you're probably convinced that unforgiveness is a Soulcrusher that's got to be defeated in your life. But you're also probably thinking I'm going to say that the way to defeat unforgiveness is to forgive. Of course, that's true, but that's like saying to conquer your fear of heights you need to start by skydiving out of a plane at 15,000 feet.

It may do the trick, but it's a tremendous first step.

So here's what I suggest. You start to defeat unforgiveness first by deciding to surrender. Surrender is the opposite of control. It's stepping back, hands up, and dropping all that you've been holding onto. That may be the prison bars you've erected, the hurts that you are clutching, the feelings you feel when you think about or see someone, and even surrender to your own ideas about how a person should act. You've got to surrender it all before you can move out of the prison and into freedom. Here's where you start.

You Don't Know What Someone's Been Through

Every person is shaped by their story. There may be other stories like yours, but your story is yours alone. Some people grow up in idyllic settings living idyllic lives, others scrape and claw and struggle every step of the way. You have no way of knowing what another person has gone through to get where they are today. You may know some of the story, but you don't know how they feel inside. Everyone carries feelings, emotions, and scars on the inside, and these things often play a role in shaping their actions.

Surrender starts when you admit that you don't know everything about the person who hurt you. Just as you hold some things back, so do they. I'm not suggesting everyone bare their souls and let it all out. But I do believe you have to reframe your vision (and therefore understanding) of the person who hurt you.

At the risk of sounding cliché, what would Jesus see when he looked at that person? They, too, feel hurt. They, too, bring expectations into the relationship. You may have hurt them and didn't even realize it. Every part of a person's past has an effect on their present and future.

Open up your mind to that, and it changes the dynamics of the relationship.

You Don't Know What Someone is Going Through Now

Ever have a bad day? What's it like to be around you on your bad days?

If you have any kind of self-awareness at all, you know when you're not in the best place. Our bad behavior isn't a mystery to us, but someone else's bad behavior often is. We judge ourselves by our intentions, but we judge other people on their actions. You never know what another person is going through. Again, it isn't always just the things you can see; it's often the things that you can't see: emotions, feelings, mood, etc.

Surrender means we give people space to feel what they are feeling and go through what they're going through. We allow them time to deal, and we try to see things through their eyes. I know you may not want to do this, but if your goal is to grow as a human and become more like Christ, it's critical. And guess what? It might just make you a little easier to get along with, too.

What if Compassion is the Goal?

Another thing those prison bars of unforgiveness block is our ability to share compassion. It's hard to give a hug to someone in prison. The bars get in the way. But compassion for another person, especially one who has hurt you, is healing. It breaks down walls and rebuilds trust. It seeks out the similarities and overlooks the differences. It builds the common ground and restores relationships.

What if that's the goal? This world has plenty of angry, intolerant people. What if you chose to be patient and understanding? It won't change the world, but it might change *your* world. It also might start a chain reaction of which *you* are the catalyst.

Learn to Love Better

At its core, forgiveness is about learning to love better. Unforgiveness is about withholding love and stoking hate. It's really as simple as that. We all want to be loved and accepted for who we are, warts and all. I know I'm not perfect, and I do things to hurt those I love. But I hope that they love me enough to know my *true* heart and to see when I'm acting out of my true character or when I'm just a broken person living in a broken world.

I also hope that I'm able to do the same thing for others. The people in my life aren't perfect, and they make mistakes. I carry some scars and wounds of their making. But it's in my best interest to forgive, open the door of the prison, and walk out those prison walls into the world with love in my heart. It is a process, but it is possible.

REPLACING UNFORGIVENESS WITH SOMETHING BETTER

What if we looked for the best in others instead of the worst?

Remember, you'll find what you're looking for if you look hard enough. But a simple way to change your thinking is this: *What would people see if they looked for the worst in me?* When you put it that way, it hits close to home. I am intimately aware of each of my flaws; I just hope that other people aren't looking too closely.

Keep that mindset when you try to work on the Soulcrusher of unforgiveness.

Look for the good in people. See where they get it right more than where they get it wrong. Allow those things to color your viewpoint of them, and then for goodness sake, get out of that prison.

You don't belong there, and you're better than that. Let it go.

The exercise below may help you move from unforgiveness to surrender to forgiveness. Think about the things that constantly cause you to hold on to past hurts and use the five steps below to release the shackles that are holding you hostage.

Acknowledge:

I struggle with unforgiveness. Each day I stay locked in the prison because of these people/situations: ______________________________ ______________________________ __________. This is a choice that I make in the morning. No one forces it on me; it is my choice.

Decide:

I will face moments today when I will struggle with unforgiveness. When this happens, I will have to decide what to do. I can either give into this and allow them to consume my mind and strengthen my cell, or I can refuse to allow the thoughts to have any power over me and place my trust in God.

Deflect/Defer:

Instead of choosing unforgiveness, I will choose surrender. I accept that we are broken people in a broken world. I acknowledge that I can choose to act or react to my circumstances. I will remember that God has redeemed me and called me by name. His hand guides my steps, and His power guards over me. His promises are mine. He has given me talents, skills, and abilities that are unique to me. I may go through difficult times, but I won't go through them alone. Today I will trust God's provision, love, and care over me, and I will share that love with the people in my life.

Reflect:

Today, I struggled with ____________________

____

____

____________________*. In spite of my struggle, I survived. I was able to do what I needed to do. Tomorrow, I will be prepared for this same struggle. I won't let it control me, and I won't let it have as much power as it did today.*

Anticipate:

Tomorrow, I will likely struggle with _______________ again. I accept this and reaffirm that it is my choice as to how I react to this struggle. I can pick up that burden again, or I can cast it off and relieve it of its power over me. I will not give it that power; it has no place in my life. I will call upon the mighty power of God to protect me and deliver me through whatever tomorrow brings.

ACTION STEPS

1. **RATE** your level of unforgiveness on a scale of 1 to 10. How often does it affect you?

2. **TAKE** a moment to reframe your thinking when it comes to the people you've been unable or unwilling to forgive. Don't replay every incident, but fast-forward through them and open up to the possibility that there's more to the story than you realize.

3. **FIND** a quiet place and take some time to think about the people you need to forgive. You'll never let go of this Soulcrusher if you aren't honest with yourself about its effects. It may help to journal a list of the relationships that need work.

4. **START** with surrender. What do you need to let go of before you can move toward forgiveness? Next to each person's name, write one or two things that you should let go of.

5. **LOOK** for the best. Write a list of all of the good things about that person or that relationship. For every negative thing you think of, write down at least two positives.

6. **GIVE** yourself permission to feel your feelings. Hurt is real, no matter what the circumstances that caused it. Surrender isn't about not feeling the pain; it's about letting go of the things that imprison you so you don't stay in the pain.

7. **COMPLETE** the affirmations above.

QUOTES

To Upend Unforgiveness

"Forgiveness is the fragrance the violet sheds on the heel that has crushed it."

MARK TWAIN

"The weak can never forgive. Forgiveness is the attribute of the strong."

MAHATMA GANDHI

"To err is human; to forgive, divine."

ALEXANDER POPE

"Forgiveness is not an occasional act; it is a permanent attitude."

MARTIN LUTHER KING, JR.

"To be a Christian means to forgive the inexcusable because God has forgiven the inexcusable in you."

C.S. LEWIS

"Forgiveness is the name of love practiced among people who love poorly. The hard truth is that all people love poorly. We need to forgive and be forgiven every day, every hour increasingly. That is the great work of love among the fellowship of the weak that is the human family."

HENRI J.M. NOUWEN

"As I walked out the door toward the gate that would lead to my freedom, I knew if I didn't leave my bitterness and hatred behind, I'd still be in prison."

NELSON MANDELA

7

DON'T WASTE TIME ON JEALOUSY. SOMETIMES YOU'RE AHEAD, SOMETIMES YOU'RE BEHIND. THE RACE IS LONG AND, IN THE END, IT'S ONLY WITH YOURSELF.

Mary Schmich

Little kids are funny. Unencumbered by societal expectations, impossible to embarrass, and not quite understanding just how the world works, they act on instinct and impulse. If they think something, they say it. If they want something, they take it.

Have you ever seen a group of kids playing in a room full of toys?

There may be Barbie dolls, Hot Wheels cars, stuffed animals, Legos, figurines, rubber balls, costumes, a dollhouse, and a mountain of other toys to play with, but watch what happens. As soon as one kid takes a strong interest in a particular toy, it becomes a magnet for the other kids.

One by one, like lions sensing the presence of a zebra on the African plains, their attention turns. Some creep stealthily forward to see this particular toy in action. They need to scope out the situation and see if the toy's current owner can somehow be enticed to give it up willingly. Others take the bold approach. They toddle with as much swagger as you can master while wearing a saggy diaper, firmly take hold of the toy and pull, while saying, "MINE!"

In the ensuing drama, all the attention turns to that amazing toy. Even the kids who were quietly and contentedly playing are suddenly interested. *What is this amazing toy that everyone wants? Why am I not over there staking my claim?* The swagger kid makes off with the toy, a victorious conqueror. He'll play with it for a few minutes and then discard it like yesterday's garbage. The same conquest for toy supremacy will take place again tomorrow in the epic struggle to satisfy that basic human desire for more.

In kids, it's funny to watch. In a room of hundreds of used, chipped, slobbered on, and bedraggled toys, there's an endless amount of entertainment. But all that matters is *that kid has something I want.* When kids become adults, it's not as funny to watch because the implications are much more serious. You can't exactly march over to someone and take their Lexus, beautiful home, or attractive spouse. That's called grand theft auto, breaking and entering, and kidnapping. These aren't as innocent as stealing someone's Barbie doll or Transformer.

So why can't we outgrow this childish mindset?

The Comparison Trap

Jealousy is a comparison trap.

It makes you examine yourself—your height, weight, appearance, hairstyle, muscle tone, bank account, career, car, house, social media following, passport stamps, dinner last night, clothing, singing voice—and compare it to someone else.

The beauty of this world is that we are all different. Jealousy makes you think we should all be the same. Defining yourself by someone else's standards is a crippling way to live.

In the mid-2000s, a Harvard grad student wrote a paper that used an acronym that you've probably heard of: FOMO. Fear of Missing Out. This means that you are bothered that something may be going on somewhere and you are not a part of it, or even worse, you've been excluded. As you can imagine, social media only adds fuel to the fire of our imagination.

Ultimately, jealousy requires you to spend all your energy thinking of what other people have instead of remembering what you have. Here's a simple truth: *someone will always have more than you, and someone will always have less than you.*

Somewhere there's a guy driving a Corvette, and somewhere there's a guy on a bicycle. Somewhere there's a guy with a lush head of beautiful, thick hair, and somewhere there's a guy with a bad combover. Somewhere there's a guy with a huge bank account, and somewhere there's a homeless person panhandling for change.

You can look at every single possession and play this same game.

Comparison gets you nowhere except frustrated.

Jealousy knows this and keeps those fires of discontentment burning brightly.

THE DOWNSIDE OF JEALOUSY

No one *wants* to feel jealous or envious. If you've ever felt this way, you know this. It's not fun to be in constant comparison mode. It sucks the joy out of your life and makes what you have seem dull. So before you can crush jealousy, you have to understand what it is and what it does to you. Only then can you cast it aside and move to a better mindset.

Jealousy Blinds You to Your Blessings

Not everyone would agree with this statement, but I believe we are all uniquely blessed. We each have a light to shine and a path to walk, and if we do it right, we can find our blessings. If you can read this, you're blessed more than most.

Think about it. You can read. That means that you have an education. Someone somewhere took the time to teach you to read and write and digest information. You can think. You don't buy a non-fiction book to be entertained; you buy a non-fiction book to digest the information and act on it. This means that you also have a desire to improve. You want the promise of this book in your own life. You want to discard Soulcrushers even if you don't yet know how. You have an income. This means you have skills that others will pay you for. You have enough money to buy a book, read it, and put it to use.

You probably don't go to that level of analysis on everything, but you could. Maybe you should. Jealousy blinds you to your blessings. It makes you focus on what you don't have or can't have yet instead of what you do have.

Jealousy is an Excuse to Do Nothing

It's amazing to me how willing most people are to lie to themselves. I'm in this category too. We lie to ourselves because we are looking for someone else to blame for our problems. So we say statements that begin with *yes, but*... I would eat healthier, but my wife keeps buying cookies. I would take time to be with my teenage daughter, but she's always on her phone. I would go throw the football with my son, but my boss has me working late tonight.

No matter what the excuse, it always comes from one place—a lack of personal ownership.

Jealousy uses these same excuses with us, so we do nothing to improve. Jealousy makes us lazy. It's much easier to scroll through Instagram and *look* at exotic places than it is to get to work, save money, and visit those places yourself. If you're a person of faith, you know that there is an enemy that wants to keep you discontented and lazy. Then you add to the strife in the world. It's hard work to take ownership of your life and do something about it. It requires self-awareness and knowing your strengths and weaknesses.

Then you've got to put those strengths to work and *get busy living.*

Here's a personal example that might illustrate my point. This book is a project I started thinking about on March 28, 2018. As I edit this chapter, it's December 4, 2020. Yeah, *that* 2020.

To say it's been a crazy year is an understatement. Naturally, I intended to finish this book a long time ago, but I got in my own way.

I could be jealous of other people who have published books this year and had great success.

I could offer lots of excuses for how other things kept me busy.

But ultimately I know the problem. I haven't been as disciplined as I needed to be to accomplish my goal to finish this book. So I have a choice: wallow in jealousy and self-pity, or get up early tomorrow and the next day and the next and keep writing. It's easy to sit there and do nothing, but that won't get you where you want to go.

Jealousy is a Partner With Pride

Jealousy is a partner with pride. I've got a whole chapter on pride coming up, but for now, consider this. Pride is a me-first attitude. It's all about what you deserve, and it's very vocal about why you deserve it. It is highly-focused but in the wrong direction. Pride and jealousy make a good pair. One looks outward at all you deserve; the other looks inward and reminds you why you deserve it. Neither does anything about your imagined predicament except keep you stirred up and unsettled. Pride combined with jealousy tells you that you deserve something—the career, the bank account, the car, the spouse—even though you've done nothing to deserve it.

It's a petty mindset that kills your joy. It also makes you very lonely. After all, who would want to be around someone who is both prideful and jealous? That's not a recipe for a fun time.

It's important to make a distinction here. Pride is different than confidence, and jealousy is different than ambition. Used properly, confidence and ambition can be very good traits. This is doubly true if you combine them with the right motivation.

It's a good thing to discover and hone your strengths and put them to work for you and the world. That's why we have innovation and improvement.

It's a good thing to have ambition. A desire to make yourself better improves marriages, relationships, vocations, and other human interactions. When you serve others out of your skill sets and help them improve, it improves you, too. Stop seeing what others have that you don't. Instead, focus on what you can become and set about to make that happen.

Jealousy Fuels Self-loathing

There are a lot of people who just don't seem to like themselves. Perhaps it's the comparison trap that shows them all the things they are not, but more likely that's jealousy talking. Jealousy fuels self-loathing. When you are constantly focused on others, it keeps you from finding happiness and contentment in yourself. You stay bogged down and stuck, never moving forward, never growing. You don't like yourself, and it shows.

CRUSHING JEALOUSY

There isn't much good to say about jealousy, but if you can overcome it, you can turn its energy into a positive. Ambition is a good thing and often a catalyst for growth and change. So consider how to overcome jealousy by doing these things.

Redefine Your Expectations

Unrealistic expectations can be killers. They set incredible standards that are often unattainable. Combined with comparison, expectations can be crippling. To crush jealousy, the first thing you must do is redefine your expectations. Your expectations should match who you are as a person. We are not homogenous. We each have different desires, hopes, and dreams. For some, it's a big bank account, world travel, and prestige. For others, it's a spouse that loves them, a warm home, and the laughter of children.

Your expectations should be yours, not a copy of someone else's.

With the wrong expectations comes a misplaced focus. You chase something that you really don't even want because jealousy tells you it would make you happy. Redefining your focus turns your focus away from what you don't have and puts it squarely on what you do.

Expectations can be fuel for your ambition, but make sure they align with how you are wired and what you were meant to do. One of my first job interviews after graduating from college with a business degree was with a financial services company. They told me I'd be working 80+ hours a week for the first two years and then be making a six-figure income. The six figures sounded enticing to me as a 22-year-old just entering the workforce, but I was getting married in three months and also wanted to build my marriage. There's nothing wrong with working hard and making a lot of money if that fits your expectations. But for me, it didn't align with my goals, so I went in a different direction.

To kill jealousy, make sure your expectations align with what brings you joy. Sometimes fancier toys just bring bigger problems. Know who you are; know what you value, and you can align your expectations to the end result. It's easy to be discontent with where you are if your target keeps moving.

Discover Gratitude

Every day of my life that goes by makes me more aware of the importance of gratitude. Jealousy short circuits gratitude. It focuses on what you don't have and makes you forget about what you do. The Oxford English dictionary defines gratitude as "the quality of being thankful; readiness to show appreciation for and to return kindness."

Thankfulness and kindness are two things that seem to be in short supply in the world today. What if instead of scrolling through social media and looking at all the things you don't have, places you've never seen, and people who look so put together, you were to write a list of things you are grateful for?

Many people talk about the power of making a gratitude list each day. It's an exercise that reframes your viewpoint. Of course, most of the days of your life aren't spectacular in the typical sense. You do the same routine over and over. It involves eating, sleeping, going to work, talking to your family, taking the kids to sports or music practice, paying bills, etc. Much of that is not social media worthy no matter how impressive the filter.

But gratitude means you look at normal everyday things differently.

If you had to write a list of ten things you are grateful for on a typical day it might include things like warm flannel sheets on a cold night. Seeing the first daffodil pop up in the spring. The tingle you got when holding your wife's hand that reminded you of when you were dating. The sound of your child's laughter. The smell of freshly-baked bread. A memory that takes you back to a special time and place. A song that makes you think of childhood.

When you look for ways to be grateful, you'll find a treasure trove of opportunities. Each one pushes jealousy down deeper and deeper and reminds you that others could easily be jealous of you.

No matter where you are in life or how bad things seem, there is always something to be grateful for—you just have to train yourself to find it.

Work Harder

Speaking of jealousy, I follow the actor Dwayne Johnson, aka The Rock, on Instagram. He seems like a genuinely nice guy. (Cue the "You're Welcome" song from the Disney movie *Moana*.) Mr. The Rock ends a lot of his social media posts with the hashtag: #HardestWorkerInTheRoom. When you look at his physique and his ability to seemingly turn any movie into a blockbuster success, it's easy to imagine he *is* the hardest worker in the room.

Jealousy is a liar that makes you think there's an easier way to get what you want. There's not. It takes hard work to have 7% body fat and killer abs. It takes hard work to put a million dollars in your bank account. It takes hard work to pay for a trip to Hawaii. It takes hard work to have a marriage that is strong and vibrant.

The lesson is this: if you want something, make it happen.

Don't waste time bemoaning what you don't have; figure out what you want, and go after it.

I love this quote by Fulton J. Sheen: "Jealousy is the tribute mediocrity pays to genius." I don't want to be mediocre in any area of my life, so I know that

I'm going to have to engage in some hard work in order to improve. It's a constant process that won't ever stop. When you get your mind wrapped around that, it brings great clarity to what you need to do. Is hard work fun? Not always, but the results that you crave won't happen unless you buckle down and get to it.

REPLACING JEALOUSY WITH SOMETHING BETTER

Jealousy is selfish, lazy, belittling, and, quite frankly, beneath you. It's an excuse to stay put, and here's a secret: staying put is never an option. You'll regress if you aren't striving to move forward. Forget about what other people have, and focus on what you have and what you can achieve simply by being you. I promise you, it's enough. Know who you are; let go of jealousy, and move forward. It will make everything in your life better.

This exercise below may help you move from jealousy to contentment. Think about the things that constantly cause you to be jealous and use the five steps below to release the shackles that are holding you hostage.

Acknowledge:

I struggle with jealousy. Each day I am jealous of: ______________________________. This is a choice that I make in the morning. No one forces it on me; it is my choice.

Decide:

I will face moments today when I will struggle with jealousy about ________________. When this happens, I will have to decide what to do. I can either give in to this feeling and allow it to consume my mind, or I can refuse to allow this to have any power over me and place my trust in God.

Deflect/Defer:

Instead of choosing jealousy, I will choose contentment. I accept that there are circumstances beyond my control. I acknowledge that I can choose to act or react to these circumstances. I will remember that God has redeemed me and called me by name. His hand guides my steps, and His power guards over me. His promises are mine. He has given me talents, skills, and abilities that are unique to me. I may go through difficult times, but I won't go through them alone. Today I will trust God's provision, love, and care over me.

Reflect:

Today, I struggled with jealousy. In spite of my struggle, I survived. I was able to do what I needed to do. Tomorrow, I will be prepared for this same struggle. I won't let it control me, and I won't let it have as much power as it did today.

Anticipate:

Tomorrow, I will likely struggle with jealousy again. I accept this and reaffirm that it is my choice as to how I react to this struggle. I can pick up that burden again, or I can cast it off and relieve it of its power over me. I will not give it that power; it has no place in my life. I will call upon the mighty power of God to protect me and deliver me through whatever tomorrow brings.

ACTION STEPS

1. **RATE** your level of jealousy on a scale of 1 to 10. How often does it affect you?

2. **SPEND** some time thinking about the comparison trap. To whom are you most likely to compare yourself? Why do you think this is the case?

3. **CREATE** a gratitude journal. Take some time each evening to write down ten things you are grateful for from that day. Challenge yourself to do this for 21 days.

4. **THINK** of one area in your life where you desire improvement. What have you done to make it happen? How can you work within your circumstances to make small improvements in the direction you want to go?

5. **SPEND** some time thinking about what you want for your life. Many times we become jealous because we are trying to live someone else's life. Define your expectations and then you have a worthwhile target.

6. **UNDERSTAND** your excuses. We all have excuses that keep us from getting where we want to go. What are your excuses? Be honest with yourself and write them down. Examine them one by one and determine which ones are laziness and which ones are legitimate. Create a plan to overcome the legitimate obstacles.

7. **COMPLETE** the affirmations above.

QUOTES

To Jettison Jealousy

"The jealous are troublesome to others, but a torment to themselves."

WILLIAM PENN

"To cure jealousy is to see it for what it is, a dissatisfaction with self."

JOAN DIDION

"Jealousy is simply and clearly the fear that you do not have value. Jealousy scans for evidence to prove the point—that others will be preferred and rewarded more than you. There is only one alternative—self-value. If you cannot love yourself, you will not believe that you are loved. You will always think it's a mistake or luck. Take your eyes off others and turn the scanner within. Find the seeds of your jealousy, clear the old voices and experiences. Put all the energy into building your personal and emotional security. Then you will be the one others envy, and you can remember the pain and reach out to them."

JENNIFER JAMES

"O, beware, my lord, of jealousy; It is the green-ey'd monster, which doth mock. The meat it feeds on."

WILLIAM SHAKESPEARE, OTHELLO

"In westerns, you meet a hardy bunch of characters. There is no jealousy in such pictures."

JOHN WAYNE

"Jealousy is the tie that binds, and binds, and binds."

HELEN ROWLAND

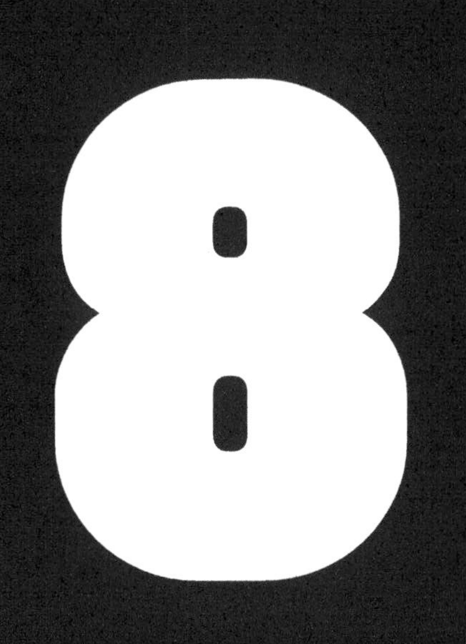
8

SQUASH SELFISHNESS

SELFISHNESS IS THAT DETESTABLE VICE WHICH NO ONE WILL FORGIVE IN OTHERS, AND NO ONE IS WITHOUT HIMSELF.

Henry Ward Beecher

In 1839, Robert Cornelius started a craze that has changed the way we view the world.

In 2002, a group of Australian friends first coined the word that described the action.

In 2003, Sony would develop a phone with a front-facing camera for video calls.

And in 2010, with the release of the iPhone 4, the front-facing camera would become the norm for smartphones. But what pushed it over the top was the rise of Instagram in 2011 with its filters and easy shareability of pictures.

In 2013, the word "selfie" was included in the online Oxford English Dictionary.

Robert Cornelius's black and white daguerreotype was now here to stay.

The selfie had arrived.

Selfishness Need Not Be Taught

People don't need a reason to be selfish. It's baked right in from birth.

As children, we think the world revolves around us, probably because it does. Children wouldn't survive without someone to take care of them. But some people fail to outgrow that childish phase. I know there's nothing wrong with selfies; I've got plenty of them with my wife and kids on my phone.

But they do point out an interesting quirk of humanity—we are all dying to be noticed.

Who's On First?

In some regards, selfishness can be understood. You *should* be your biggest cheerleader and push yourself to be and do your best. There are a lot of voices in the world that will push you down, make you feel bad, and use you up. The loudest voice in your head should be the one telling you to get up, move forward, and be awesome.

Hopefully, when you look in the mirror you see all the things that make you awesome instead of all the things that make you average. There's also the well-known analogy of the oxygen mask on an airplane. As the flight attendant gives the speech that you ignore because you've heard it a hundred times before, she's making a valuable point.

Sometimes you've got to take care of yourself *before* you can help others.

If you are a wreck, you won't have anything left to give.

However, there is a tipping point in life and on a plane. Putting on your own oxygen mask, then reclining your seat and watching the chaos all around isn't acceptable. Neither is taking care of yourself to the exclusion of all others. You may get what you want in life, but you'll find yourself in a very lonely place.

The trick is to find balance. If you've read any of my books or articles, you know that I'm a firm believer in self-improvement. I believe we are most valuable to the world when we are growing, evolving, and becoming better versions of ourselves. For believers, that means being conformed to the image of Christ. But everyone can improve, and in that improvement, we find ways to bring others on our journey. Since "a rising tide lifts all boats", when we get better, we can't help but make others better too.

THE DOWNSIDE OF SELFISHNESS

There's a funny scene from an episode of the TV show *Friends* where Joey (the somewhat dim-witted but lovable goof) goes on a date with a woman. She keeps reaching across the table and taking bites of his meal. He's getting more and more frustrated until finally he snaps and says, "Joey doesn't share food!"

My wife and I joke about this because I'm kind of like that, too.

When we go out to eat, my wife will always ask if I want to try some of her meal. On the other hand, when my plate arrives, I dig in and make it a personal challenge to make all my food disappear. My wife is welcome to try anything she wants on my plate, but it's up to her to come get it before it's gone! Over the years, I've gotten better at sharing, and I use this illustration humorously, but selfishness run amuck isn't an attractive quality, although it may be our natural tendency.

Selfishness Limits Your Potential

Every person comes from different backgrounds, socioeconomic levels, races, genders, and nationalities. We all have different and unique stories that shape us and make us who we are. But selfishness stunts your story. It limits your potential. I believe we all carry seeds of greatness. The end result is going to look different for everyone, but we all have a part to play. Your part is interconnected to mine and everyone else's.

Selfishness halts your growth as a person.

You may be full-grown and look like an adult on the outside, but inside every selfish person is a child. Just like a child is not going to win the Olympics, be elected president, drive a car, start a family, start a company, or any other thing that defines success, neither will you if you stay completely selfish. People will begin to see you for what you are, and your opportunities will shrink.

Ironically, by turning your focus inward, you limit your scope, and your world shrinks.

Selfishness is a Relationship Killer

Here's a riddle: which came first, selfishness or loneliness? It's kind of like the age-old question about the chicken and egg. Selfishness makes you lonely. When you continually use people, they start to notice. It doesn't take long before they get wise to the fact that you give much more than you take. Soon they start dropping off or finding excuses not to be around you. Relationships only work when you have a healthy balance of give and take.

Selfishness is a Paradox

A few years ago, I worked on some projects with Zig Ziglar's organization. Zig died in 2012, but his children are carrying on his message. Zig was an author, speaker, and salesman with a message of positivity who believed people could be, do, and have more if they were willing to work for it.

One of Zig's best-known quotes is, "You can have everything in life you want if you'll help enough other people get what they want." This paradoxical statement reveals part of the problem with selfishness. It seems that by looking out for #1, you are on the fast track to getting what you want.

The reality is that looking out for others is a more effective means to personal success.

Much of my vocational writing takes place in the online and entrepreneurial world. I write the words that help other people clarify their message and refine what they're trying to say. For each of my clients, I start by helping them create great content, in line with their message and brand, and give it away. Maybe it's articles, videos, free guides, tools, access to a course; it doesn't matter what it is exactly—what matters is that they help a person who could benefit from the message. Then something starts to happen. More and more people start talking about the message. They move from strangers to fans. And then from fans to customers. In many cases, these customers tell us what they need and ask us to create it and sell it to them!

Zig called this his core secret. If you find out how to serve and help others, they'll help you back. As selfish as people can be, this, too, is human nature. So what do you want? Help others first, and you'll be surprised at what you get back in return.

CRUSHING SELFISHNESS

As a Soulcrusher, selfishness is deceptively light.

Picking it up daily doesn't seem to be a burden because it comes so naturally. But its effects over the long term are surprisingly heavy. Perhaps you've felt some of them yourself and want to put down that load and walk in selflessness. It is possible. It starts with how you view others.

Become a Servant

There's a well-known story in the gospels where Jesus exhibits what it means to be a servant. Gathered with his disciples in the upper room, and knowing that he'll be arrested, beaten, tortured, and killed in a number of hours, Jesus shows what it means to love and serve others.

The Bible says he takes off his outer garment, stoops down with a towel and a basin of water and a rag, and begins to wash his disciples' feet. Now, I'm going to pause there for one minute. Some feet are cute, but first-century dude feet, not so much. These calloused feet covered in dust and grime from walking across the countryside.

They probably smelled bad and felt worse.

But Jesus loved his disciples.

Just like a parent loves their children and will overlook any level of gunk and grime, Jesus took the place of a slave and began washing their feet. Can you imagine the scene in the upper room? Twelve disciples meant twenty-four feet and two hundred and forty toes. That's a lot of nooks and crannies. I'm sure some of the disciples were uncomfortable as they waited for their turn. But in the end, Jesus had shown them that no matter what your position (Son of God included), you aren't above loving—and serving—your fellow man.

You want a cure for selfishness, here it is: serve others.

You don't have to look far to see a world full of hurting people. It doesn't have to be as drastic as bending down to wash the dirty feet of another. It can be any simple act of service. But serving does something for the servant and the served. It connects you and melts your selfish heart.

Put Yourself in Your Place

If you want to crush selfishness, you also have to put yourself in your place. We all have a tendency to think we're the best there is. It's good to have self-confidence and know your strengths and where you excel, but don't let it go to your head.

Selfishness causes you to begin to look down on others. You may not vocalize it, but it can become a running commentary in your head. In Romans, Paul taught that you must stand apart from the world by changing the way you think. Just after these verses, in Romans 12:3, he writes, "Do not think of yourself more highly than you ought to think." His purpose in the next section is to remind believers that every person has a part in the story. This part is one that only they can play.

Selfishness renders your part greater than anyone else's. It makes you believe that you are more important than others. Every person has a critical part to play. Put yourself in your place, and help others play their part to perfection.

Empty Yourself

There's a beautiful passage in Philippians where Paul demonstrates how Jesus emptied himself of his divinity so that he could come to earth and become a servant of all mankind. It's an interesting concept to think about emptying yourself or pouring out all you've got.

We tend to be hoarders instead.

Did you ever play the game *Hungry, Hungry Hippos* when you were a kid or when your kids were young? The object is to gobble up as many marbles as possible. That's kind of what we do in real life. We consume more and more because that selfishness comes naturally. But then what happens is we have no room for anything else, even if that anything else is better for us than what we've so carefully hoarded.

Jesus reminds us that becoming more like him means we let go of all that we think we need. We open our hands and stop clutching the things of this world. We stop thinking about what we deserve and instead start thinking about how to help others get what they deserve. We paradoxically put them first, and by association, we start to see improvements in our own life. It's a counterintuitive way to think, but emptying yourself leads to fullness of another, more lasting kind.

REPLACING SELFISHNESS WITH SOMETHING BETTER

As long as you live you'll battle selfishness. It's that simple. But making a decision to put others first is a habit that can be learned, just like any other. It just takes conscious effort and a willingness to trust that you'll be better off for it. This exercise below will help you move from selfishness to selflessness. Think about the areas in which you are selfish and use the five steps below to begin thinking less of yourself and more of others.

Acknowledge:

I struggle with selfishness. Each day I pick up my selfishness in these areas: ____________________
____.
This is a choice that I make in the morning. No one forces it on me; it is my choice.

Decide:

I will face moments today when I will struggle and put my needs over all others. When this happens, I will have to decide what to do. I can either give into my selfish nature and put myself first, or I can choose to help others.

Deflect/Defer:

Instead of choosing selfishness, I will choose to serve others. I accept that there are circumstances beyond my control. I acknowledge that I can choose to act or react to these circumstances. I will remember that God has redeemed me and called me by name. His hand guides my steps, and His power guards over me. His promises are mine. He has given me talents, skills, and abilities that are unique to me. I may go through difficult times, but I won't go through them alone. Today I will trust God's provision, love, and care over me.

Reflect:

Today, I struggled with ___________________

____

____

__________. In spite of my struggle, I survived. I was able to do what I needed to do. Tomorrow, I will be prepared for this same struggle. I won't let it control me, and I won't let it have as much power as it did today.

Anticipate:

Tomorrow, I will likely struggle with _______

____

____

again. I accept this and reaffirm that it is my choice as to how I react to this struggle. I can pick up that burden again, or I can cast it off and relieve it of its power over me. I will not give it that power; it has no place in my life. I will call upon the mighty power of God to protect me and deliver me through whatever tomorrow brings.

ACTION STEPS

1. **ON** a scale of 1 to 10 rank your selfishness level. One means you serve others often and put their needs ahead of your own. Ten means you look out for Number 1 all the time.

2. **WHAT** is one area of strength for you that you could use to help others? Find someone who can benefit and help them—quietly, and with no expectation of anything in return.

3. **WHAT** are some things that you need to empty yourself of to make room for something better?

4. **THINK** about the people you will interact with this week. Pick one person and decide to put their needs first. Bring them coffee, ask their opinion, listen before talking, etc.

5. **WHAT** is the part of the big story that you were called to play? If you weren't so concerned with being first, best, or noticed, what would that enable you to do in your life?

6. **COMPLETE** the affirmations above.

QUOTES

To Squash Selfishness

"Manifest plainness, Embrace simplicity,
Reduce selfishness, Have few desires."

LAO TZU

"Self-absorption in all its forms kills empathy, let alone compassion. When we focus on ourselves, our world contracts as our problems and preoccupations loom large. But when we focus on others, our world expands. Our own problems drift to the periphery of the mind and so seem smaller, and we increase our capacity for connection—or compassionate action."

DANIEL GOLEMAN,
Social Intelligence: The New Science of Human Relationships

"Almost every sinful action ever committed can be traced back to a selfish motive. It is a trait we hate in other people but justify in ourselves."

STEPHEN KENDRICK,
The Love Dare

"Great achievement is usually born of great sacrifice and is never the result of selfishness."

NAPOLEON HILL

"Every man must decide whether he will walk in the light of creative altruism or in the darkness of destructive selfishness."

MARTIN LUTHER KING, JR.

"As selfishness and complaint pervert the mind, so love with its joy clears and sharpens the vision."

HELEN KELLER

"Our world is drowning in a sea of self-centeredness. You can make yourself quite unique right away by leaving this ocean of selfishness and choosing to be curious about other people."

JOHN BYTHEWAY

"If you wish to travel far and fast, travel light. Take off all your envies, jealousies, unforgiveness, selfishness and fears."

CESARE PAVESE

9

PRIDE MUST DIE IN YOU, OR NOTHING OF HEAVEN CAN LIVE IN YOU.

Andrew Murray

I used to have a big problem with pride, and I'll be honest, it kind of surprised me.

Pride didn't ever seem like a big issue to me.

Growing up, I was a pretty quiet kid. I did well in school, but I didn't really stand out all that much. I was kind of in the middle. I wasn't popular; I wasn't picked on. I didn't do sports, and I wasn't that competitive.

I just did my thing and graduated with good grades and moved on to the next phase of life.

Trophies and awards didn't drive me; I simply had an internal drive that pushed me to do my best and to the best of my ability, do everything with excellence. To me, pride was the loudmouth person who couldn't help but shout from the rooftops how awesome they were. In school and in life, I knew lots of people like that, but that was never me. I never particularly felt prideful because I didn't really care if anyone knew about me or not.

Or so I thought.

Beware of Besetting Sins

Pride took on a whole new light for me because of a sermon series Ronnie Kendall, my pastor at the time, did on Hebrews 12:1 which says, "Therefore, since we are surrounded by such a great cloud of witnesses, let us throw off everything that hinders and the sin that so easily entangles. And let us run with perseverance the race marked out for us…"

In this message series, Ronnie talked about the concept of besetting sins. That's basically the King James (the 1500s King James, not the basketball version we have today) way of saying *trips up, entangles, hinders.*

Over the course of a few weeks, Ronnie explained that there are three main sins that people struggle with: *pride, unforgiveness, and fear.* A little bell went off in my head as he unpacked this sermon series.

I wasn't particularly fearful; I was young then and felt invincible.

I didn't really have a problem with unforgiveness; people make mistakes and we move on.

But pride. Oh man, as he laid it out, pride was a totally different story.

Who's In Charge?

I've been a professional writer now for just over five years, but I've been honing my craft all my life. When you introduce yourself as a writer, people always ask the same question: *what have you written?*

You may not think about it, but everything that you read was written by someone. That includes all the books, articles, emails, advertisements, signs, reviews, songs, you name it. If it contains words on a page, there's an often unnamed writer behind those words.

Much of what I've written I can't tell you about.

Not because it's top secret and I'll have to kill you or anything, but because it's *for* someone else. I've developed the skill of being able to interview people of all age ranges, races, and genders and helped them write their story. Through my written words, I've been a sixty-something white man in politics, a fifty-year-old female African American former executive for Coca-Cola Enterprises and Frito Lay, a sixty-plus year old African American man who runs a nonprofit organization in Washington D.C., a young couple high up in multi-level marketing, and multiple business owners and leadership coaches.

This makes it hard to answer the question: *what have you written?*

Most people think of writers as people who write books, like the one you're holding now.

What's this have to do with pride? Plenty.

It turns out my problem with pride wasn't about being *the best*, but it was about being *seen*.

Every writer—myself included—wants to see their name on the cover. You created something, so it's only natural to want the world to know.

Want that enough, and guess what you've got?

Pride.

It took me a lot of years to realize this was an issue in my life. Looking back, I realize that God needed to work that out of my system before I could move into the work He created me to do. It took me many more years to be okay with helping others bring their message to life, even if I get none of the credit. Now, I'm honored to be able to do so. I believe it's a gift God has blessed me with and one I honor him by using daily. Sometimes God refines us by putting us in a place where we have no other choice but to push through to the lesson on the other side.

And guess what? Now I feel confident enough to write my own books with my name on the cover and not have it go to my head. That's what happens when you crush pride.

THE DOWNSIDE OF PRIDE

Pride is a tricky Soulcrusher because if you are like me, you might not even realize it's an issue. Unlike some of the others, it doesn't seem to really hurt you that much. To be sure, if you are that jerk who is the *best* and *knows it*, that can be off-putting to people. But if you are that person, then you are probably too busy winning, no matter the cost, to care how other people see you. But if you, like me have a subtler version of a pride problem, here's what can happen.

Pride Gives Too Much Credit

In professional football (the American kind), there is one player who typically makes the most money on the team—the quarterback. The quarterback has his hands on the ball every single time it's snapped. Only the center has as much responsibility.

The quarterback's job is immense, and he's often the engine behind the offense. He has to know which play to call and make sure his offense is lined up correctly. He's got to read the defense, and based on what he sees, make sure the play he's called is still the right one. While this is going on, the play clock is winding down. He's only got forty seconds to make sure everything goes off according to plan. When the center snaps the ball to the QB, it's a signal for the offensive pieces and parts to snap into action.

It's also a signal to the defense to attack.

Suddenly, his five three-hundred-plus pound offensive linemen are blocking a tidal wave of similarly-sized defensive linemen. The second wave of defensive tackles, smaller by fifty or so pounds, but lightning-quick, try to break through, disrupt his throw, and drive the quarterback to the ground before he can get rid of the ball.

If a quarterback plays well on any given Sunday, he looks like a genius.

He reads and exploits the defense and puts the ball where only his receivers can get it. He keeps track of all the plays and scores points. In the end, he's a large part of the reason his team wins.

But if the quarterback doesn't play well...he's a bum. He can't make the throws. He gets intercepted. His team is playing catch-up, and in the end, he's a big part of the reason his team loses.

On Monday morning, fans across the country dissect his play and give him too much credit for the win and too much blame for the loss. Pride works like this. When things go right, pride puffs you up and makes you feel better than you are. In football, there are eleven players on offense every time the ball is snapped. All eleven, including the quarterback, have just as much to do with a play's success or failure.

Pride can blind you to the role others play in your success and keep you from giving credit where credit is due.

Pride Halts Your Growth

If you are a growth-minded individual who is always striving for self-improvement, when do you quit? The answer is probably never because we never reach our goal, and there is always room to get better.

Pride blocks that growth.

It convinces you that you are better than you really are or that you've gotten as good as you're going to get. It may feel good to quit striving in the long run, but in the end, you'll just slide backward or be passed up by someone who didn't quit.

When your self-awareness is high, you look out for potential blind spots and areas for growth. In my friend Greg Cagle's book *Be Weird: Succeed in Life and Business Simply By Being You*, he talks about the need to look for blind spots. He calls these overused strengths.

Pride blinds you to the fact that your strengths can be overused and therefore sometimes abused. When this is the case, it can cause devastating consequences to your growth and your relationships with others.

Pride Hurts You and Hurts Others

Have you ever met a know-it-all? This type of person is always right and never wrong.

Ask a question, and they know the answer.

Answer a question wrong, and they feel the need to correct you.

This is pride in action. The Soulcrusher of pride is like a self-defense mechanism. It can kick in to make you look better, be righter (is that a word?), sound more confident, have a louder opinion, and generally just be obnoxious.

The bad part—*you often can't even see it.*

Frankly, I struggle with this sometimes. I make a living with my brain, and consequently, I read and study and know a lot of stuff. This can make me feel like I always have to say something when, in actuality, there are plenty of times I need to just keep my mouth shut.

It feels good to be right, but when being right damages other people, it's not so good. Pride may make you feel like you need to be on top, but it can lead to collateral damage, and that collateral damage can hurt others.

Pride Goes Before a Fall

When I was growing up, my best friend's dad raised horses and mules. The horses were easy to ride. Throw on a saddle blanket, cinch up the saddle, slip on a bit and bridle, make sure the stirrups were the right length, and you were good to go.

The mules served a different purpose.

They would be harnessed to pull a wagon. I still don't understand how all the rigging worked, but the one thing I remember was the blinders on the bridle. The blinders made it impossible for the mules to look anywhere but straight ahead. There's a good reason for this. You don't want a ton and a half of mules hooked to a wagon to see something out of the corner of their eyes, get spooked, and take off. It's one thing to control a horse from the saddle; it's quite another to control a big animal hooked to a wagon.

Sometimes pride puts blinders on us.

We can only look straight ahead, and we don't see the consequences of our pride sneaking up on us until it's too late. Proverbs 16:18 says, "Pride goes before destruction, a haughty spirit before a fall." You see it all the time. The leader who let his pride get in the way of his common sense, and before long—he steps off the cliff, and down he goes.

CRUSHING PRIDE

Pride seems different because it is. Unlike some of the other Soulcrushers, pride *can* have some beneficial side effects. It can make you succeed and look like a success. It can help you accomplish great things. It's not all bad, but it must be managed, or it will get out of control. If you want to crush pride, you've got to do a few things.

Be Honest

It's nice to be first, but the truth is no one is *the best* at everything. If you are serious about reducing pride, you've got to be honest with yourself. Know who you are, and know who you aren't. This equips you to look for help where it makes sense to do so.

Acknowledge those who came before you. We all stand on the shoulders of others. Give them credit for their help, and you reduce your pride and self-dependence.

There's not much more humbling than asking for help. But this is good for your soul.

The very act of asking someone to help is good for them as well. Chances are the areas where you are weak are areas where someone else is strong. Humility gives them a chance to shine and helps you keep your pride in check.

Give Credit to Others

Another way to crush your pride is to give credit to others. We all have a desire to be seen and known for our contributions. If you struggle with pride, you can make sure *other* people are seen and heard. This can look a lot of different ways.

If you are a boss in charge of people, you can give shout outs to the team when they do something that helps everyone succeed. Going back to the quarterback analogy, this is what great QBs do. If you are a parent, you can make sure your kids know you recognize it when they do something great. If you are married, tell your spouse that you recognize a sacrifice they've made or something they have done for your family.

Taking more than your share of the blame when things go wrong, and less of your share of the credit when things go right, is a hallmark of people who keep their pride in check.

Know Your Place

When I was a teenager, an acquaintance of mine a grade or two above me quoted something called *Fellowship of the Unashamed* from memory. It made a huge impact on me. I'm not sure of its origins, but it's often attributed to an African pastor who was later killed for his faith. It's a declaration of what his faith meant to him, including the desire to put his own selfish desires aside in order to grow closer to God and stronger in faith.

Here's the part that stands out to me now in light of the crushing burden of pride:

> *I no longer need pre-eminence, prosperity, position, promotions, plaudits, or popularity.*
>
> *I now live by presence, lean by faith, love by patience, lift by prayer, and labor by power. My pace is set, my gait is fast, my goal is Heaven, my road is narrow, my way is rough, my companions few, my Guide reliable, my mission clear.*
>
> *I cannot be bought, compromised, deterred, lured away, turned back, diluted, or delayed.*

To paraphrase John the Baptist: "I must decrease so that he can increase." Here's the deal—if you want to be used *by God* and *for God*, you've got to crush your pride. You've got to know your place. You must be second so God can be first.

The irony is that when you reach this place, God will often elevate you higher and farther than you could have imagined. The difference is that now you can actually enjoy it because it's His handiwork, not yours.

Pride is powerful, but surrender opens doors you never even knew were there.

REPLACING PRIDE WITH SOMETHING BETTER

This exercise below may help you move from pride to humility. Think about the things that constantly cause you to puff up with pride, and use the five steps below to release the shackles that are holding you hostage.

Acknowledge:

I struggle with pride. Each day I allow these things to fill me with pride: ______________________

____.

This is a choice that I make in the morning. No one forces it on me; it is my choice.

Decide:

I will face moments today when I will struggle with pride. When this happens, I will have to decide what to do. I can either give in to my pride or give up my pride for something better. I refuse to allow pride to have any power over me, and I place my trust in God.

Deflect/Defer:

Instead of choosing pride, I will choose humility. I accept that I must be second so God can be first. I will remember that God has redeemed me and called me by name. His hand guides my steps, and His power guards over me. His promises are mine. He has given me talents, skills, and abilities that are unique to me. I may go through difficult times, but I won't go through them alone. Today I will trust God's provision, love, and care over me.

Reflect:

Today, I struggled with ____________________ ________________________________. In spite of my struggle, I survived. I was able to do what I needed to do. Tomorrow, I will be prepared for this same struggle. I won't let it control me, and I won't let it have as much power as it did today.

Anticipate:

Tomorrow, I will likely struggle with ________

____

again. I accept this and reaffirm that it is my choice as to how I react to this struggle. I can pick up that burden again, or I can cast it off and relieve it of its power over me. I will not give it that power; it has no place in my life. I will call upon the mighty power of God to protect me and deliver me through whatever tomorrow brings.

ACTION STEPS

1. **RATE** your level of pride on a scale of 1 to 10. How often does it affect you?

2. **WHAT** are the gifts and abilities that make you successful in the world? List as many as you can think of here. Now evaluate how often you take credit for those things. How many are you doing on your own, and how many are from God working in you?

3. **COMMIT** to recognizing and encouraging others this week. Each day look for someone who has done something amazing and tell them you recognize their contribution. Compliment them and encourage them to keep going. This takes the focus off of you and puts it onto another.

4. **LOOK** for sneaky pride. In what ways does pride hide out in your life? Think about places where pride may be blinding you to areas in which you can grow, and make a plan to root it out.

5. **COMPLETE** the affirmations above.

QUOTES

To Pummel Pride

"A proud man is always looking down on things and people; and, of course, as long as you are looking down, you cannot see something that is above you."

C.S. LEWIS,

Mere Christianity

"All men make mistakes, but a good man yields when he knows his course is wrong, and repairs the evil. The only crime is pride."

SOPHOCLES,

Antigone

"Pride gets no pleasure out of having something, only out of having more of it than the next man... It is the comparison that makes you proud: the pleasure of being above the rest. Once the element of competition is gone, pride is gone."

C.S. LEWIS,

Mere Christianity

"There is no one who would not rather appear to know than to be taught."

QUINTILIAN

"The proud person always wants to do the right thing, the great thing. But because he wants to do it in his own strength, he is fighting not with man, but with God."

SOREN KIERKEGAARD

"We are rarely proud when we are alone."

VOLTAIRE

"God opposes the proud, but gives grace to the humble."

JAMES 4:6

"Most of the trouble in the world is caused by people wanting to be important."

T. S. ELIOT

"It is better to lose your pride with someone you love rather than to lose that someone you love with your useless pride."

JOHN RUSKIN

"First pride, then the crash—the bigger the ego, the harder the fall."

PROVERBS 16:18, THE MESSAGE

10

DEMOLISH DISAPPOINTMENT

WEALTH CONSISTS NOT IN HAVING GREAT POSSESSIONS, BUT IN HAVING FEW WANTS.

Epictetus

The best all-you-can-eat buffet I ever gorged on was one June morning at the Tusker House restaurant at Disney's Animal Kingdom. There were several reasons why it was so good. First, my daughter had been on a youth mission trip for the week, and meeting her that day for brunch was the first time we'd seen her in a while. Sharing a meal together is always a great way to reconnect.

The second reason it was so good was because of my wife's killer planning skills. She'd done her research and she found out that if you made your reservation for

10:45 A.M. you would be able to have both breakfast items *and* lunch items.

Boom! You instantly double your value (which is important when paying Disney prices.)

I'm pretty sure I speak for most dads when I say this next part.

Dads are interesting creatures.

We invented phrases like, "Shut the door—were you born in a barn?"

"You're letting all the bought air out."

"Turn that light off if you aren't using it."

Most dads hate waste. That's what makes buffets so interesting and provides a good backdrop to a chapter on disappointment. At every buffet I've ever been to, I always leave feeling terrible.

Why?

Because I'm determined to get my money's worth. If I don't, I'll leave feeling disappointed.

So I go back again and again for food that I no longer need because I was stuffed three plates ago. I get dessert just because it's there and eat until I'm way past satisfied.

When you don't stop when you are satisfied, this is what happens.

And this is why disappointment is a Soulcrusher.

Disappointment is essentially the opposite of contentment, gratification, or satisfaction.

For many of us, we struggle with disappointment because we've never defined what it would take to be content and satisfied. So, like a person who paid for the all-you-can-eat buffet, we are determined to leave no dish untasted and wring every last bit of value out of our purchase.

The problem is we push way past full and wonder why we are miserable.

Are You Feeling Satisfied?

At its core, disappointment comes because we don't know what it means to be satisfied.

On one hand, this drive forward is good. It pushes us to learn and grow. It forces us out of our comfort level and causes us to take risks. It makes us look to the future and hopefully plan for a better tomorrow.

The trick is knowing when to stop or, at the very, least slow down.

Life can make us feel like we're on a hamster wheel. We jump on when we go through the typical motions that are universally accepted—make good grades in school so you can go to college. Get a degree in college so you can get a job. Get a job so you can make money. Make money so you are an attractive potential spouse or can buy cool toys. Get married so you can start a family. Use your money to buy a house, some cars, and keep the cycle going. Raise your kids so they can start the cycle all over again.

Obviously, I'm exaggerating the point, and I know it sounds a little cynical. I don't mean it that way, but

I want to draw attention to the fact that most people jump on the hamster wheel and start spinning without ever considering what they want in life.

They never define what it will take for them to be satisfied.

So when and if they do "succeed", they are stunned when they feel so disappointed.

Behind the Scenes or Highlight Reel?

On top of that, we live in a time where we are more digitally connected than ever. We are bombarded with social media posts and advertisements that make us jealous because everyone else looks so happy, so *content.*

They have it all, so what's wrong with me?

You've probably seen the memes on the internet that say something to this effect—*don't compare your behind the scenes to everyone else's highlight reel.* But that's exactly what we do. We look at pictures of perfect families without any struggle or strife, delicious meals without any calories, exotic vacations without any debt and forget that they've been polished, filtered, and finessed to show the most appealing parts of their lives.

Few people show their arguments, tears, fat rolls, failures, and doubts.

So we can't see what it took to get to that point—the reality behind the mask.

But we think *they've* got it perfect. And by comparison, *my* life is a mess.

And incrementally, with every swipe and scroll to the next post, the weight of disappointment begins to crush down on us. Our lives pale in comparison to theirs.

THE DOWNSIDE OF DISAPPOINTMENT

The truth is life is hard.

You lived through 2020, so you know about disappointment. That year thousands of us lost income and jobs; vacations were canceled; we had to mask up to go out; our kids had to do school virtually; we had to work virtually; we got used to conflicting messages from our, ahem, *leaders*; we watched a crazy election cycle spiral out of control; oh, and on top of that, hundreds of thousands of people around the world died from a virus that, at the time I'm writing this is still ravaging out of control.

Disappointment is real. It's also understandable. However, it doesn't have to rule over you.

Here are some of the downsides of disappointment if it's left unchecked.

Disappointment Focuses on the Wrong Things

Disappointment is a whiny, obnoxious baby because it puts your attention on the wrong things. It makes you look at what's missing from your life rather than what you have right in front of you. It's a glass-half-full kind of viewpoint that always assumes you *deserve* more or better.

It's not hard to fuel disappointment when this is your mindset. If you want to crush disappointment, you must learn how to change your thinking and learn to look at the world differently.

In reality, every day is a gift.

Most days I wake up and quickly tell God, *thank you for the breath in my lungs and the beat of my heart.* Disappointment is arrogant. It tells us we *deserve* something other than what we have.

We don't.

If you are reading this book, you are probably better off than half the people in the world. You can read, so you can learn. You have disposable income to buy this book, so you probably have enough money to take care of the bills. Treat each day as a gift and begin to focus on the blessings right in front of you, and you won't have time to focus on what you don't have.

Disappointment Overlooks the Blessings You Have

If I came to your house, what would I find? If I followed you to work, what would people say about you? If I asked your friends to tell me what makes you great, what would they say?

Disappointment tells you your house is too small, your work is unimportant, and you are overlooked. The truth is more complicated than that. Every person has blessings in their life—they just have to look for them.

It's almost trite, but that's why the quote, *I cried because I had no shoes until I met a man with no feet* is so pertinent. No matter how high you climb in life, there will always be someone who is one step farther than you. There are also plenty of people who are many steps behind you. Perspective is key, but disappointment blinds you from a proper perspective on your own life.

If you are being crushed by disappointment, it may just be time for an attitude adjustment and a new perspective. Learning to look at your life differently helps you see the blessings you have in a new light.

Disappointment is Fueled By Comparison

We live in a time where it's easier than ever to compare our lives to the lives of others.

It's fertile ground for disappointment.

Comparison is the fuel that keeps disappointment growing. It blinds you to the good in your life while highlighting the good in everyone else's. So when someone posts a picture of themselves on a vacation, you get jealous because you aren't there. (Never mind the incredible vacation you took a few months ago.) When someone is excited about their new promotion, you bemoan the fact that you had to work late last night.

Comparison is a thief of joy. It robs you of the happiness you could have for people and replaces it with jealousy and disappointment in your own life. If you want to crush disappointment, you must decide to stop comparing yourself to others and create standards that are unique to your own hopes and dreams.

CRUSHING DISAPPOINTMENT

We get disappointed because we have ambition, hopes, dreams, and goals. I don't have to tell you that life doesn't always work out as planned. We both know that from painful experience. But sometimes what you hoped for isn't even the best thing for you. Sometimes what happens is even better. I'm sure you've had some experiences like this too. Crushing disappointment doesn't eliminate it—hurts still hurt—but it does reframe disappointment in a way that provides contentment and satisfaction no matter what the circumstances.

Redefine Expectations

One of the driving forces behind disappointment is your expectation. It makes sense right? If disappointment is truly something that happens inside of you, your expectation is the cause. When you *expect* a certain something to happen, and it doesn't, it's no surprise you become disappointed.

The problem is that we put expectations on events over which we have no control.

I can't control the weather, the whims of others, or the weight of the world on my shoulders.

The trick to overcoming disappointment is to redefine your expectations. I'm not saying you should be like Alexander Pope who said, "Blessed is he who expects nothing, for he shall never be disappointed." A life with no expectations would be dreary indeed. I'm not interested in just surviving life, and neither are you. I want to thrive. That's why you can revise your expectations so they are more realistic and give you room to enjoy life.

In other words, you don't make your expectations *lower*, you make them *better*.

When it comes to what you expect out of life, you can try a more serendipitous approach. Remind yourself that life is an adventure to be lived and a journey to be enjoyed. Train yourself to expect the unexpected, and then roll with it when it happens.

For relationships, you have to take a different approach. Author Donald Miller says, "When you stop expecting people to be perfect, you can like them for who they are." Expectations are killers in relationships because one person usually has no idea what the other one *expects*. So naturally, they can't live up to an expectation they don't know is even there.

Recognize that people are vastly different from one another. Redefine what you expect from those in your life. Make a habit of looking at the positive, unique, and different things about the people in your life and you can better understand and appreciate them.

Make a Gratitude List

Another way to combat disappointment is to make a gratitude list. We often remember the bad things that happen because they cause us pain. It's like going out for a meal and complaining when our food doesn't come out just right. We expect it to taste good, but we rarely compliment the chef when it does.

A gratitude list is a way to reframe your day or week in light of the positive things that give you hope. It's easy to do. At the end of each day, just spend some time listing some things you are grateful for. Write them down in a journal so you can keep a running track of all that's good in your life.

When you do this often enough, you have a written record of how blessed your life really is. This record can be a disappointment-buster that changes how you view the world. Philippians 4:8 says, "Whatever is true, whatever is noble, whatever is right, whatever is pure, whatever is lovely, whatever is admirable—if anything is excellent or praiseworthy—think about such things."

Disappointment causes us to dwell on the bad things.

Gratitude reminds us of all we have that is good.

Evaluate What You Need to Be Content

We each have a measuring stick we use to determine the quality of our lives. For some, it's the amount of money in their bank account, the number and type of cars in their garage, the extravagance of their vacations, or the size of their house. For others, it's the number of followers on their social media feeds or the number of likes their posts get. For others still, it's the depth of their relationships, the warmth of a snugly built house, or a dinner with friends.

When we measure our lives by someone else's measuring stick, we are sure to get disappointed. That's why it's critical you are sure you are measuring the right things.

You do this by determining what you need to be content. Back to the buffet example above; if one plate of food fills you up, the second and third may be there for the taking, but they'll only make you miserable.

When you know how much is enough—in life, in love, in finances—you can stop looking when you find fullness. Then you can shift to adding richness and depth to those things. You pay the bills and are content with your life. You invest in yourself and others so you bring meaning and quality to your relationships. You are generous with your finances, using them as a tool to help others.

Contentment, once defined, is easy to attain; it's the antidote to hopelessness.

Be a Blessing to Others

It's hard to be disappointed in your own life when you are busy blessing others.

If you are struggling with disappointment, sometimes it helps to take the focus off of your own life and put it onto another. This can mean taking tangible actions like giving to a cause you care about or volunteering your time to help out others.

I recently heard about a local church that was using the Christmas season to help an organization called Jambos that provides pajamas to kids in foster care. They rallied their members and asked them to buy PJs for kids. It's hard to be down on your own life when you think about kids away from their families at Christmas who don't have fun pajamas.

When you bless others, it lightens your load. It reframes your difficulties and puts them into perspective. It may not solve your problems, but it can change your outlook.

Bringing joy to someone else's life tends to increase the joy in your own.

REPLACING DISAPPOINTMENT WITH SOMETHING BETTER

Disappointment is something we will continue to face because life in a broken world is challenging. But learning to let go of this Soulcrusher can help you live a better life and be a blessing to others.

This exercise below may help you move from disappointment to contentment. Think about the things that constantly cause disappointment and use the five steps below to release the shackles that are holding you hostage.

Acknowledge:

I struggle with disappointment. Each day I pick up these cares and they overwhelm me: ________

____

____. This is a choice that I make in the morning. No one forces it on me; it is my choice.

Decide:

I will face moments today when I will struggle with disappointment over _______________. When this happens, I will have to decide what to do. I can either give in to disappointment and allow it to consume my mind, or I can refuse to allow disappointment to have any power over me and place my trust in God, His blessing and provision.

Deflect/Defer:

Instead of choosing disappointment, I will choose trust, faith, and contentment. I accept that there are circumstances beyond my control. I acknowledge that I can choose to act or react to these circumstances. I will remember that God has redeemed me and called me by name. His hand guides my steps, and His power guards over me. His promises are mine. He has given me talents, skills, and abilities that are unique to me. I may go through difficult times, but I won't go through them alone. Today I will trust God's provision, love, and care over me.

Reflect:

Today, I struggled with ____________________. In spite of my struggle, I survived. I was able to do what I needed to do. Tomorrow, I will be prepared for this same struggle. I won't let it control me, and I won't let it have as much power as it did today.

Anticipate:

Tomorrow, I will likely struggle with ____________________________ again. I accept this and reaffirm that it is my choice as to how I react to this struggle. I can pick up that burden again, or I can cast it off and relieve it of its power over me. I will not give it that power; it has no place in my life. I will call upon the mighty power of God to protect me and deliver me through whatever tomorrow brings.

ACTION STEPS

1. **RATE** your level of disappointment on a scale of 1 to 10. How often does it affect you?

2. **LIMIT** your intake of social media. Social media is a comparison trap. Research has shown that it increases feelings of loneliness and sadness. Consider purging your social media and paring down who you follow to only those people who add value and contentment to your life. At the very least, set limits for how much time you'll scroll.

3. **CREATE** a gratitude journal. Challenge yourself to spend a few minutes each evening writing down three things you are grateful for today. Big or small, it doesn't matter. The idea is to simply look for goodness in your life.

4. **DEFINE** what contentment looks like to you. Take some time to evaluate what you are measuring in your life. Are they things that make you feel content, or are they someone else's hope, dreams, and goals? Realign what you need to be content, and pursue that with abandon.

5. **COMPLETE** the affirmations above.

QUOTES

To Demolish Disappointment

"Blessed is he who expects nothing, for he shall never be disappointed."

ALEXANDER POPE

"If we will be quiet and ready enough, we shall find compensation in every disappointment."

HENRY DAVID THOREAU

"We must all suffer one of two things: the pain of discipline or the pain of regret or disappointment."

JIM ROHN

"The principles of living greatly include the capacity to face trouble with courage, disappointment with cheerfulness, and trial with humility."

THOMAS S. MONSON

"Trying to design the perfect plan is the perfect recipe for disappointment."

PATRICK LENCIONI

"True happiness is to enjoy the present, without anxious dependence upon the future, not to amuse ourselves with either hopes or fears but to rest satisfied with what we have, which is sufficient, for he that is so wants nothing. The greatest blessings of mankind are within us and within our reach. A wise man is content with his lot, whatever it may be, without wishing for what he has not."

SENECA

"Happiness is not a goal...it's a by-product of a life well-lived."

ELEANOR ROOSEVELT

"He who is not satisfied with a little is satisfied with nothing."

EPICURUS

"You say, 'If I had a little more, I should be very satisfied.' You make a mistake. If you are not content with what you have, you would not be satisfied if it were doubled."

CHARLES SPURGEON

"It isn't what you have or who you are or where you are or what you are doing that makes you happy or unhappy. It is what you think about it."

DALE CARNEGIE

"Many people lose the small joys in the hope for the big happiness."

PEARL S. BUCK

"For after all, the best thing one can do when it is raining is let it rain."

HENRY WADSWORTH LONGFELLOW

"We need much less than we think we need."

MAYA ANGELOU

11

HALT HOPELESSNESS

WE MUST ACCEPT FINITE DISAPPOINTMENT, BUT NEVER LOSE INFINITE HOPE.

Martin Luther King, Jr.

Hope is both incredibly fragile and delightfully resilient.

But when it's tested, it often pushes us to our limits.

How much could you take before you lost hope?

Imagine you were a collegiate track star who set records and competed in the Olympic games, traveled across the ocean on a ship to compete, set a record for the fastest lap time in your discipline, but didn't win the gold?

Would that shake your hope?

What if seven years later, as an Army Air Corpsman in the middle of the biggest war the world had ever seen, your plane was shot down in the middle of the Pacific Ocean, leaving you stranded in a rubber life raft with two of your crewmen, one of whom would die from his wounds?

Would that shake your hope?

Imagine spending the next forty-seven days in a liferaft, trying to survive by remembering your survival training, waiting for a rescue that might never come. When you do see a boat on the horizon, you get as excited as your weakened state will allow. With the last bit of your strength, you wave your arms to get someone's attention.

Your spirits lift because rescue is near!

But when it gets closer, you get a sinking feeling in the pit of your shrunken stomach—it's flying the flag of the Japanese Navy, your enemy. The ship gets close enough to fish you out of the water and bring you aboard the ship. For the first time in over a month, your feet are on solid ground, but your nightmare is just beginning.

Would that shake your hope?

You are transferred to the Japanese mainland. Then, for the next two years, you are beaten, tortured, starved, spit upon, brutalized, isolated, and forgotten in a Japanese prisoner-of-war camp. Your family receives a letter that you are dead.

How much hope would you have left?

Most of us would have zero to none.

This isn't a made-up story to illustrate a point; it's the story of Louis Zamperini. A USC track athlete, he competed in the Berlin Olympics in 1936. A proud American, he fought in WWII and survived years at the hands of a sadistic prison guard. He could have collapsed and crumbled. No one would have been surprised nor even blamed him.

And yet...

Through some spark of divine hope, he endured.

Even more, after an encounter with the Holy Spirit at a Billy Graham revival in 1949, he forgave his captors and committed his life to God.

Sometimes even in the darkest of days, hope finds a way to shine.

Shades of Gray

Few people have a life story as painful as Louis Zamperini's first thirty or so years. But that doesn't mean that you don't struggle with hopelessness from time to time. It also doesn't minimize your story. This final Soulcrusher is one that affects everyone at some point or another. It is universal.

Not all hopelessness is the same; it comes in shades of gray.

For some, it's when things don't go as planned, and they feel the emptiness of broken dreams. For others, it's the loss of a loved one who died too soon. It may be the gut-punch of a broken marriage or the disappointment of a wayward child, the loss of a job or the death of a pet, the broken heart of first love lost.

Hopelessness isn't one-size-fits-all.

But it feels the same, nonetheless.

At its core, hopelessness is a blow to your vision—both of what is and what could be. It clouds clarity and slips a pair of dark glasses over everything you see. Whenever your particular shade of hopelessness darkens your vision, the causes don't matter because the pain is all the same.

But just like a fire starts with a single spark, hope can be a spark that pierces the darkness and rages into an inferno.

Out of Control

Perhaps the worst part of hopelessness is the feeling that you are alone.

God created us for relationship—both with Him and with each other.

Hopelessness takes that away.

It isolates and separates; it makes us feel like we have no one by our side. This is something that the enemy uses mercilessly. He feeds on that separation and loneliness, and like an incessant dripping of water, makes you feel like you are all alone. In this loneliness, despair can set in.

Through our darkened view of the world, we then start to see things not as they are, but as hopelessness tells us they are. We feel unloved and disconnected. We feel unmotivated and out of control. Every difficulty seems too big. Every problem is insurmountable.

Worst of all, it's contagious.

Hopelessness rubs off, and it takes a strong person to withstand its pull.

THE DOWNSIDE OF HOPELESSNESS

One of the things that's a hallmark of my writing is its ability to encourage.

I realize that ending this book on hopelessness could be a bit of a downer, but stay with me. In life sometimes you've got to go through the valley before you can stand on the mountaintop, and this chapter is no different. We're going to walk through the valley of hopelessness, but I promise I'll take you to the mountaintop before we're through.

Hopelessness Makes Work Feel Futile

I believe it's safe to say that unless you are a sociopath, you want to be a good person. I think everyone does. We may disagree on what, exactly, *good* looks like, but most people try to do the right thing more often than not.

Most people also believe that there is some sort of higher power or divine force—God—that sets the rules and gives us something to strive for. So we go about our lives trying to do our best, all the while wondering if our best is going to be good enough.

All belief systems, save one, are built upon doing good works. Work hard enough, be *good* enough and you have a shot at making God happy. Hopelessness makes this work seem futile. The bad news is that, on your own, your work *is* futile. In Isaiah 64:6, the Bible says, "We are all infected and impure with sin. When we display our righteous deeds, they are nothing but filthy rags. Like autumn leaves, we wither and fall, and our sins sweep us away like the wind." (NLT)

We look at our good works—the way we treat others, the things we build, the money we amass—with pride. It feels like such an accomplishment. So, like toddlers bringing finger paint drawings to their teacher, beaming with pride we say, *look at what I made!* We hope this will gloss over all the times we treated others poorly, built things selfishly, and pursued stuff with greed.

Deep down we know that no matter how much we strive, our work will never be enough to get us to God, so we lose hope.

Hopelessness Makes Worry Constant

If 2020 taught us anything, it's that we have far less control over things than we'd like. Through the COVID19 pandemic, we have learned a lot about ourselves and how tenuous our grip on life is.

And this has caused worry to blossom like a weed.

When we don't have hope, we default to worry. It's not surprising, because without hope, our eyes bounce to the closest threat and fixate upon its power to do us harm. So we pick up our bag of worries each day, or as Jesus alludes to in Matthew 11:30, we pick up the wrong yoke and struggle under its burden.

Like being chained to one of those big iron balls from the cartoons, we can't move forward, backward, nor to the side more than a few feet either way. Our progress grinds to a halt, and our strength withers. This leaves us feeling helpless and alone. Like a virus, the worries we carry seem to multiply and attract other worries. It's like a chain reaction that becomes our constant companion.

As the worries pile on, the light of hope dims.

Hopelessness Makes Your Future Seem Scary

When you think about the future, what do you see?

Without hope, the future is scary, and understandably so. If the past is any indication, the future isn't so bright. There's no reason to think that people are going to get any less selfish toward one another. Wars will still happen. Diseases will still rage. History will keep repeating itself until we finally are no more.

And then there's death. (Stick with me here, I promise we'll be out of this valley soon.)

Without hope, death is the scariest mystery of all because it's such an unknown.

Death is final and formidable. It's indiscriminate and takes those we love.

I know this from painful experience. You probably do too.

We do our best to ignore this and live our lives as fully as possible, but work and school and bills and hurt feelings and trouble rob us of much of the joy we could have as we march ever closer to the end. Then, when we lose someone we love, we are often filled with regret over lost time and painful feelings and words.

So we bury ourselves in a present that seems futile, running from a past that is painful, and into a future that is uncertain. Busyness is our defense, and we give it all we've got.

Hopelessness Makes the Darkness Seem Impenetrable

What's the darkest place you've ever been? I mean literally, not figuratively.

One time I had to travel to Orlando, Florida from my home in Atlanta, Georgia for a quick business conference. The following week, my family and I had plans to head to the beach for a week's vacation on the Gulf Coast. I booked a one-way flight to Orlando and planned to rent a car and drive to meet my family after my trip was over.

When my conference ended, I caught a ride back to the airport with my friends Jason and Charlie. They hopped on a plane to head home, and I picked up my rental car. By about seven p.m. I was on the road to points north and west.

By the time I reached the panhandle of Florida, it was long past dark.

There are some desolate stretches of land when it's near midnight and you are in the middle of nowhere. I was driving down one particular backroad, stands of pine trees pushing up against me on either side, and the road stretching straight ahead like an unrolled spool of black ribbon, when I looked up and caught a glimpse of the stars.

It hit me that I should pull over, turn off my headlights, and simply look up.

So I did.

I pulled off on the shoulder and turned off the ignition. I flipped my headlights off and stepped out into the warm Florida night. I could hear the sounds of insects in the woods and the ticking of the car engine. I circled around to the front of the car and slid to a seat up on the warm hood. I leaned back and stared up at the stars.

It was one of the most beautiful sights I'd ever seen.

I could see the sparkling band of the Milky Way Galaxy stretching out before me.

All around me, the woods were inky black. The night sky was like velvet. But those pinpricks of light from the stars sparkled as bright as anything I'd ever seen.

Hopelessness makes everything seem as black as that forest. It blinds you to what's possible and forces your head down. But when you remind yourself that there is hope, that there is light beyond the darkness, all it takes is a spark, and the world opens up before you, and hope floods in like the light of a galaxy so big it has to be measured in light-years.

CRUSHING HOPELESSNESS

Whew. All right, are you still with me?

I told you we had to walk through the valley before we get to the mountaintop, and that valley gets tough sometimes. Hopelessness is a beast. It's the worst Soulcrusher of all because it sits there like a heavy weight on your chest. It pushes you down until you literally cannot move. However, there is hope, so here is how you crush hopelessness once and for all and move into the burning light of hope.

Hope Comes When You Lower Your Defenses

Part of the beauty of the way God created us is our desire to strive, push forward, and grow. It's what's led to innovation, knowledge, and exploration, and it's helped us thrive. But it also has a dark side. We want to be in control at all times.

This means we sometimes put up walls that block us off from others.

We show the world a version of ourselves that may be sometimes true, but it hides our warts and imperfections. This allows us to hide, but it also contributes to our isolation and loneliness. And this is where hopelessness thrives.

One of the best, although paradoxical, ways to build hope into your life is to lower your defenses and embrace authenticity and vulnerability. To be sure, this takes courage. Not everyone will like the real you. However, those that do will be drawn to your ability to be true to who you are and to show how you are growing.

When you are willing to be vulnerable, it shows people that you don't have it all together. It's one of the traits I try to exhibit in my writing. Even as I write these words, I have doubts about whether or not they are any good. It's why this has taken me two-plus years to get to this point.

But eventually, I had to decide to put it out there and let you, the reader, be the judge.

Some people will love this book and its message; some won't.

Ultimately, I don't really care either way. I believe it's a message God has given me, and I trust Him to make sure the right people read it and *hopefully* are blessed. My walls are down, and my message is out. That gives me hope.

Hope Is Maximized When You Find a Friend

Hopelessness is the fungus of the Soulcrushers. It breeds in the dank darkness and hangs out alone. Hope needs a friend. It needs someone to share your burdens, prop you up when you are weak, and encourage you to be strong.

If you want to find hope, find a friend.

The good news is if you are authentic about where you are struggling and where you are growing, it won't be hard to find people in a similar place. We are all works in progress, and where you may struggle, I may be strong. And vice versa. When we lean on each other as we walk toward the finish line of life, we create and carry a spark of hope.

This spark is contagious.

It's why we cheer when we see the video of the little boy in karate class struggling—and then ultimately overcoming—his inability to break a board. Or why we get tears in our eyes when we see the track athlete stop her race to help her injured competitor cross the finish line.

Hope is best shared with others.

Hope is Refined When You Look to God

It's hard to have hope when your head is down. The view of the ground is not that exciting, and each step forward (if you are moving at all) feels pitifully inadequate. But hope grows when you look up.

Specifically, when you look up to God.

Because of God's radical love for you, He became the hope of the world. He recognized that without Him we would face a problematic past—so He provided purity in forgiveness. He knew that we would have a futile present—so He provides peace in the storms. And He knew that we would face an uncertain future—so He gave us the hope of Heaven.

Hope lifts your eyes and moves them from what is behind toward what is coming.

When you look to God, the dark glasses fall away as you are blinded by His light.

God is a master restorer who loves to fix broken things. He makes all things new.

This includes you.

Have you ever wondered why, in our darkest days, we turn to God?

It's because deep down we know that is the only way we can soar.

Isaiah 40:31 says, "but those who hope in the LORD will renew their strength. They will soar on wings like eagles; they will run and not grow weary, they will walk and not be faint."

We were made to soar, to do great things, and to point people's gaze to God.

When we soar with hope, it is refined, and our very lives become an inspiration.

Hope is Realized When You Rest in Christ

At its core, hopelessness is restlessness. It's the persistent suspicion that you are made for more, and yet somehow are mired in mediocrity. It's the deep-down desire for rest that restores and renews. It's being poisoned by weariness and longing for the antidote.

The only way to find that rest, that hope, is in Jesus Christ.

He came to free you from the burden of perfection that you could never bear, from the work you could never accomplish, and from a future that you could never find. He came to give you hope and peace.

When we rest in Christ, as that African pastor martyred for his faith wrote, *my past is redeemed, my present makes sense, my future is secure.* Deep down, that's what we all long for. This world is broken and will be until Jesus comes back. I'm not here to tell you that there's some magic fix to make all your problems go away.

But I do know this from personal experience:

Without Jesus, I'd be crushed under the weight of hopelessness.

With Jesus, I have the strength to keep going day after day.

He gives me rest that helps me invest in others, encourage, and strive onward.

And that rest fills me with hope.

REPLACING HOPELESSNESS WITH SOMETHING BETTER

This exercise below may help you move from hopelessness to hope. Think about the things that constantly cause you to lose hope, and use the five steps below to release the shackles that are holding you hostage.

Acknowledge:

I struggle with hope. Each day I run up against hopelessness in these areas: ____________________
____.
This is a choice that I make in the morning. No one forces it on me; it is my choice.

Decide:

I will face moments today when I will struggle with hopelessness because of ____________________. When this happens, I will have to decide what to do. I can either give in to these things and allow them to consume my mind, or I can refuse to allow them to have any power over me and place my hope and trust in God.

Deflect/Defer:

Instead of choosing hopelessness, I will choose to trust and put faith in hope. I accept that there are circumstances beyond my control. I acknowledge that I can choose to act or react to these circumstances. I will remember that God has redeemed me and called me by name. His hand guides my steps, and His power guards over me. His promises are mine. He has given me talents, skills, and abilities that are unique to me. I may go through difficult times, but I won't go through them alone. Today I will trust God's provision, love, and care over me. He fills me with hope.

Reflect:

Today, I struggled with ____________________ ______________________________________. In spite of my struggle, I survived. I was able to do what I needed to do. Tomorrow, I will be prepared for this same struggle. I won't let it control me, and I won't let it have as much power as it did today.

Anticipate:

Tomorrow, I will likely struggle with ______________________________________ again. I accept this and reaffirm that it is my choice as to how I react to this struggle. I can pick up that burden again, or I can cast it off and relieve it of its power over me. I will not give it that power; it has no place in my life. I will call upon the mighty power of God to protect me and deliver me through whatever tomorrow brings.

ACTION STEPS

1. **RATE** your level of hope on a scale of 1 to 10. How often does hopelessness affect you?

2. **THINK** about your life, and list as many things as you can that give you hope. Now, look at the list and see which ones last and which ones let you down. Is it possible that you've placed your hope in something that can never fill you?

3. **CONSIDER** how a lack of hope affects your relationships. Where might not having hope cause damage to those you love?

4. **WHERE** do you need to practice more authenticity and vulnerability? How might doing so allow you to connect with people who need hope?

5. **HOW** is your relationship with God? Consider areas where you may need to draw closer to God and put your trust in Him. What will this mean you have to give up?

6. **COMPLETE** the affirmations above.

QUOTES

To Halt Hopelessness

"Just as man cannot live without dreams, he cannot live without hope. If dreams reflect the past, hope summons the future."

ELIE WIESEL

"Hope is the thing with feathers
That perches in the soul
And sings the tune without the words
And never stops at all."

EMILY DICKINSON

"Live, then, and be happy, beloved children of my heart, and never forget, that until the day God will deign to reveal the future to man, all human wisdom is contained in these two words, 'Wait and Hope.'"

ALEXANDRE DUMAS

"And now these three remain: faith, hope and love. But the greatest of these is love."

1 CORINTHIANS 13:13

"Do not spoil what you have by desiring what you have not; remember that what you now have was once among the things you only hoped for."

EPICURUS

"Fairy tales do not tell children the dragons exist. Children already know that dragons exist. Fairy tales tell children the dragons can be killed."

G.K. CHESTERTON

"Remember, Hope is a good thing, maybe the best of things, and no good thing ever dies."

STEPHEN KING

"When you're at the end of your rope, tie a knot and hold on."

THEODORE ROOSEVELT

"If at first the idea is not absurd, then there is no hope for it."

ALBERT EINSTEIN

"Keep a little fire burning; however small, however hidden."

CORMAC MCCARTHY, THE ROAD

STAND UP

At the beginning of this book, I had you sit down and take a deep breath.

You may not have realized it at the time, but you were carrying a backpack full of burdens. They weighed on you each morning as you shouldered your load and headed out into the world. They bowed your back and slowed your stride. With a list of burdens like these, it's no wonder that you couldn't go as far or as fast as you'd like.

Who could blame you?

Look at this list.

- **FEAR** — robbed you of your confidence and caused you to live life timidly.
- **DOUBT** — took away your courage and the assurances you knew to be true.
- **ANGER** — festered until it consumed you and crippled you for life.
- **BITTERNESS** — became a byproduct of anger that captured your joy.
- **WORRY** — took away your focus on today and turned it into anxiety over tomorrow.

- **UNFORGIVENESS** — made you hang on to past wounds and relive them over and over.
- **JEALOUSY** — became a constant comparison where you couldn't be happy for others.
- **SELFISHNESS** — caused you to overlook others and only focus on yourself.
- **PRIDE** — convinced you that you are better than others and deserve more.
- **DISAPPOINTMENT** — caused you to look at the world in a negative light.
- **HOPELESSNESS** — caused you to want to give up. That's quite a load to bear. No wonder you were weighed down and unable to move.

But now, I want you to do something for me. I want you to *stand up*.

Take a deep breath, throw your shoulders back, and tell me how you feel.

My hope is that now that you know about the burdens you were carrying, burdens that were *crushing your soul*, you've been able to work through some of them. You are a work in progress, so I know you aren't there yet. But keep pushing forward.

Your load should be lighter now. That backpack isn't so heavy.

You can begin to change what you carry each day.

Here is your new load, along with a verse to encourage you each day.

- **REPLACE FEAR WITH COURAGE.** *For God has not given us a spirit of fear and timidity, but of power, love, and self-discipline.* (2 Timothy 1:7)
- **REPLACE DOUBT WITH CONFIDENCE.** *But blessed are those who trust in the Lord and have made the Lord their hope and confidence. (Jeremiah 17:7)*
- **REPLACE ANGER WITH LOVE.** *Love prospers when a fault is forgiven, but dwelling on it separates close friends. (Proverbs 17:9)*
- **REPLACE BITTERNESS WITH JOY.** *Dear brothers and sisters, I close my letter with these last words: Be joyful. Grow to maturity. Encourage each other. Live in harmony and peace. Then the God of love and peace will be with you. (2 Corinthians 13:11)*
- **REPLACE WORRY WITH TRUST.** *The Lord is my strength and shield. I trust him with all my heart. He helps me, and my heart is filled with joy. I burst out in songs of thanksgiving. (Psalm 28:7)*

- **REPLACE UNFORGIVENESS WITH FORGIVENESS.** *If you forgive those who sin against you, your heavenly Father will forgive you. But if you refuse to forgive others, your Father will not forgive your sins. (Matthew 6:14-15)*
- **REPLACE JEALOUSY WITH CONTENTMENT.** *A peaceful heart leads to a healthy body; jealousy is like cancer in the bones. (Proverbs 14:30)*
- **REPLACE SELFISHNESS WITH SERVICE.** *For even the Son of Man came not to be served but to serve others and to give his life as a ransom for many. (Matthew 20:28)*
- **REPLACE PRIDE WITH HUMILITY.** *Pride ends in humiliation, while humility brings honor. (Proverbs 29:23)*
- **REPLACE DISAPPOINTMENT WITH SATISFACTION.** *Pay careful attention to your own work, for then you will get the satisfaction of a job well done, and you won't need to compare yourself to anyone else. (Galatians 6:4)*
- **REPLACE HOPELESSNESS WITH HOPE.** *"For I know the plans I have for you," says the Lord. "They are plans for good and not for disaster, to give you a future and a hope." (Jeremiah 29:11)*

Here's the deal. I know that life can be cruel. I lost my dad to cancer several years ago. That sucks, and I miss him every day. I have two friends that are dealing with the disease now, and it isn't fair. I have regrets in life about things I could have or should have said and done better. I have expectations that didn't pan out. I've lost jobs I enjoyed. I've bounced checks and overdrawn my bank account. I've let down people I loved.

I still sometimes struggle with pride. I want to be known and make a difference in the world. I get jealous of others, even if it doesn't make any sense, and I know better. I'm selfish because it's easier just to look out for me.

I don't want you to think that I'm some Pollyanna who thinks everything is roses and rainbows. It's not. I know that, and I'd be disingenuous if I didn't admit it. But the whole idea behind this book is to recognize that there *are* Soulcrushers in the world, but *you don't have to let them rule your life.*

You have a choice. And as long as you have a choice, you can make a change.

My hope is that you see this list and realize which ones are crushing you. Then I hope you have the courage and the willingness to do something about it. Set your burden down. Call it the Soulcrusher it is, then *refuse* to pick it back up.

This isn't something that you can do just once. It must happen over and over again.

Each day you have to choose a *Soulbuilder* to go in your pack instead.

This will equip you to stand up straight, stride forward with purpose, and carry the load that leads to life. If you do this often enough, you will become the kind of person that lifts others too. So what will you do with what you've learned?

Will you fragment fear? Destroy doubt? Annihilate anger? Bomb bitterness? Wipe out worry? Upend unforgiveness? Jettison jealously? Squash selfishness? Pummel pride? Demolish disappointment? And halt hopelessness?

If you have the courage to set down that load and move forward, your life will never be the same.

Let's hit the trail.

To unpack the tools to lift you on your journey, be sure to visit SoulcrushersBook.com. You'll find an ever-growing list of reader bonuses designed to help you soar.

ABOUT THE AUTHOR

Jesse Barnett is an Atlanta-based craftsman at heart who brings stories to life through writing, speaking, coaching, and teaching. From his dad, he learned the trade of finish carpentry, and discovered the impact of taking the time to build things with precision, pride, and persistence. Now, he applies those same traits to his work as a writer where he collaborates and strategizes with others who have an idea they want to share with the world but don't trust their ability to do so.

It's precisely his diverse background—carpenter, businessman, ordained minister, and teacher—that has equipped him to connect with others to tell their unique stories in a powerful way.

His professional work includes a stint as a content writer with John Maxwell's organizations where he helped develop courses and curriculum for a number of leadership coaches and facilitators. As a collaborative book writer, he's worked with people ranging from superstars in the network marketing space, pastors of churches, leaders of non-profit organizations, and C-Suite leaders looking to teach others their leadership and personal growth skills.

An entrepreneur at heart, he's the creator of the Storyscribr course—an online course that teaches people to interview their loved ones or mentors and turn their story into a priceless book. As a craftsman and wordsmith, Jesse's goal is to weave words into stories that teach, transform, encourage and do it all with a high degree of excellence.

His greatest joy, though, is spending time laughing and creating memories with his wife Becca, daughter Julia, and son Joel, who by the way, said he should add more quirky stuff to this bio, so here you go: He enjoys going off the beaten path to find his own way—usually where it's dangerous. Which explains why on a solo camping trip he once spent the night hiding out in a tent from a black bear that found and foraged his food supplies. He won an Excellence in Writing award in Mrs. Moore's fourth grade class—but took a couple decades to realize he *was* a writer. And a few more years after that to pursue writing as a profession. Most of his vehicles have been either red or black, probably subconsciously because those are the colors of his alma mater, the University of Georgia. One day, he hopes to live on the beach but have a log cabin in the mountains (that he and his kids built together) to use as a writing retreat.

ABOUT THE AUTHOR

If you want to connect with Jesse to continue your personal growth journey, get tools for living a better life, or simply hear more of his crazy stories, visit him at BarnettWrites.com. If you're feeling really adventurous, contact him directly at Jesse@BarnettWrites.com.

Made in United States
North Haven, CT
27 December 2022